NEW ROAD

5

NEW ROAD
5

edited by

WREY GARDINER

GREY WALLS PRESS LIMITED
Crown Passage, Pall Mall
London

First published in 1949
by the Grey Walls Press Limited
7 *Crown Passage, Pall Mall, London S.W.*1
Printed in Great Britain
by Balding & Mansell Limited
London

CONTENTS

ENGLISH POETRY
chosen by Wrey Gardiner

6

ILLUSTRATIONS

ACKNOWLEDGEMENT

Mr. Derek Stanford wishes to make acknowledgements to the Hogarth Press for permission to quote from the English text of Rilke's poems and letters translated by J. B. Leishman and Stephen Spender and from *The Notebook of Malte Laurids Brigge* translated by John Linton, and to Messrs. Sidgwick & Jackson for permission to quote from their *Letters to a Young Poet* translated by Reginald Snell.

Derek Stanford

RILKE
AND HIS EXCLUSIVE MYTH

'MORE and more mankind will discover that we have to turn to poetry to interpret life for us, to console us, to sustain us. Without poetry, our science will appear incomplete; and most of what now passes with us for religion and philosophy will be replaced by poetry.'

So wrote Matthew Arnold in 1880; and if his times and their customs, both good and bad, seemed then to be in the melting-pot that process has met with great acceleration since. In the realm of conventions and collective beliefs the electric-furnace and the apparatus for splitting the atom have their counterparts—giant psychological engines, so to speak, for the manufacture of nihilism and crude political religions of power.

This being so, it is not surprising that literature and art are largely judged today, not for their formal excellence alone, but in proportion to that degree in which they contain a faith for living. From *The Bible designed to be read as literature* to literature designed to be read as a Bible one short step only was missing; and that one step has now been taken.

Granted, then, a certain mastery of form, a requisite technical ability by means of which the content of the work is conveyed with the power to persuade and convince, our chief concern will be to discover the plan for living implicit within it. This approach is not to be mistaken as one which confuses art with propaganda. Here, we expect to find no more than a demonstration of propositions according to some constant *a priori* theory; but in the message we anticipate in art we look for the fresh unprejudiced reports of the

9

free-lance sensibility; answers arrived at without consulting the book. These answers we shall estimate just in so far as they apply to our life, the success which their application achieves, the breadth and depth they are found to cover.

For us, in an age where belief is partial (concerning the Vote or Transubstantiation, but never embracing the whole field of life), we come to art for a universal meaning and read its images as a kind of catholic gloss. This meaning, perhaps, is best described by use of the term 'mythology'—implying a coherent imaginative world-picture, a non-didactic exegesis of things.

One of the first factors observed in such a study of the German poet Rilke is the private and unadulterated make-up of his myth. Unlike most poets whose verse has held a system of belief in solution, the credo to be found in the work of Rilke evolves from no extra-literary source. For Dante and the later Eliot, Catholicism has been the sure base; for Wordsworth and Shelley respectively, Hartley and Plato were the instructors; for Hölderlin, the Gods of Greece and Christ provided the twin foundation-stone; while in the 'mad' sonnets of Gerard de Nerval (who tried to believe in every religion) the names of conflicting deities are strewn like the fragments of fallen temples.

Along with William Blake, but even more unremittingly poetic—allowing even less to the claims of logic and the common insistence on an argued system—the mythology of Rilke originates in pure unforced poetic perception. In him we can study a type of revelation utterly untampered by the intellectual will; in no way distorted or made to square with any predetermined beliefs. As the reports of intuition came in, as they were newly expressed in his verse, as they were stored and resorted in his mind year after year with an eager trusting patience, so little by little a whole organum grew, value upon value came to emerge, until at the end of his true creative life, after 'the Duinese Elegies', a full inter- pretative gospel stood forth: a religion and morality essen- tially poetic.

That impersonal analytical machine patented by the Western mind and christened logic was an apparatus which Rilke never used to solve his problems. In place of this method of calculation on the scientific margin of the human page—this manner of discarding the affective situation—Rilke substituted an inward-speaking voice. 'Have patience', he wrote in his *Letters to a Young Poet*, 'with everything that is unsolved in your heart and try to cherish the questions themselves, like closed rooms and like books written in a strange tongue.' For him there existed no convenient mental adding-machines to answer life's teasers. There was no ready-reckoner accessible to all. Truth was to be come at in a private fashion; born only from an experiential relation. 'Do not search now', he continued to advise, 'for the answers which cannot be given you because you could not live them. It is a matter of living everything. Live the question now.'

Following from this, it seemed to Rilke that there was no time-limit for any of these questions. Unlike the Schoolman, who believed that by the correct employment of Reason, the right application of the proper formula, a problem might be solved in so many steps, Rilke placed his faith in patience and time; in the sure working-out of an inner growth of light. 'To be an artist', he writes in his Third Letter, 'means not to reckon and count; to ripen like the tree which does not force its sap and stands confident in the storms of Spring without fear lest no Summer might come after. It does come. It does come. But it comes only to the patient ones, who are there as if eternity lay in front of them, so unconcernedly still and far.'

At first we may wonder how such an approach, abandoning the common instrument of reason, can possibly create a mythology to furnish the need of a multitude of men. Solipsist, however, as all poets tend to be, through the intense nature of their internal life, their final unrefuted claim upon our ear is the basic human element that leaves us all kin. Just as the demagogue-opportunist addresses his appeal to the lowest common denominator in man, so the poet unconsciously or consciously feels that in answering his own personal problem he likewise provides an articulate answer to the queries of man's highest common denominator. How far this was so in Rilke's case is something we must now decide.

Poetic perception and passive will, a mind both open and obedient in recording the data of intuition: these were the agents which Rilke employed in his pursuit of truth and meaning. The matter, however, does not rest here. Another factor now enters in. Unfalsified as were these dispatches of sensibility by the intellect—by means of a conscious shaping theory, adjusting our first apprehension of things to fit some standardised cosmic account—another force was at work upon them, giving them a uniform direction and dress. Indeed, some collective girdle for our thoughts, some string to bind our separate sensations, to make from our moments of individual living a personal continuum in time and space, is necessary to each of us; and, what is more, inevitable. With Rilke, this unifying power was the instinct which led him to interpret phenomena according to the needs of his own artistic life. Setting the requirements and desires of man—of the natural male in his own make-up—under the heel of the artist in him, he inverted the outlook giving rise to most of our current human values.

The artist, thought Freud, resorts to art in order to re-adjust the balance which nature and his early years have weighted against his worldly success. Once this balance has been established and approval of women and his fellow-men gained, the need for creation becomes abated; the 'productive neurotic' approaches the normal. Such has been the lot of many creators: of Wordsworth, Rossini, and—dare one hazard—Shakespeare. To others, though, this haven is denied. Never can they return at peace to graze with the 'satisfied' human herd. Their boundaries must for ever remain outside the pastures of 'normality'. Here—either because their original neuroses were wells too deep for their art to drain, or because their creative powers were too weak to disperse their complex by its projection—they are doomed to live out their whole existence in a condition of solitude.

This, one cannot doubt, was Rilke's state; which a certain poetic pride, perhaps, a certain masochistic arrogance, a certain conscious perversity strengthened. 'The artist', wrote Novalis—that great aphorist of Romanticism—'stands on the man, as a statue stands on its pedestal'; and in every single affair of life Rilke so ordered his actions and decisions that this supremacy might be maintained: a selfish martyr who indulged his splendid gifts.

Paradoxically enough, it is these mental exiles, these creative pariahs, whose works have most enriched and modified our world by the peculiar substance of their message. Whereas the art produced by those figures who finally come to terms with life, accepting the outward conventions of men, paying their respects to popular values, may often charm us with its form, the tranquil perfection of its poise, the harmony, sweetness and peace of its tone, it lacks a dynamic urgency, that grasp on our mind which only conflict held in harmonic tension can produce. Of such a latter kind is the poetry of Rilke.

Every epoch or century, as Drucker and Chakotkin have pointed out, has its dominant concept of the human being. For the thirteenth century, man was chiefly a spiritual creature; for the sixteenth century, an intellectual creature; for the eighteenth century, an economic creature. In what light does man most regard himself today; on what aspect of his nature does he place a premium? On the sexual, answers the critic J. F. Hendry; and from the middle of the last century onwards our literature has given it a heavy underlining. For Baudelaire—along with God (so making up Original Sin)—sex was the central and ramifying theme; for Rimbaud—desiring to reinvent love—sex was the springboard and the gate, the magic passport to ecstatic truth; for Dostoievsky, it meant much more than any critic save Berdyaev in his splendid study has shown. It is hardly important to trace the matter further; for the imprint of the satyr's hoof, in some form or other, disguised or apparent, is present in most of our key modern writing: in Lawrence, Kafka, Nietzsche, Gide, Joyce, and Proust. A significant approach to the subject of sex might almost form a criterion, then, for estimating in a ready fashion the claims of a writer upon our age. (A touchstone, in fact, which Lawrence employed in *Classical American Literature*.) Under such a testing Rilke starts off well.

From the beginning he repudiates all Puritan and Catholic conceptions of sex without adopting the other extreme—a Walpurgis cult of debauchery and whores, somewhat in favour among artists of his time. Against the mortification of the flesh, and its repression preached by the Church, his poem *A Nun's Complaint* makes a poignant protestation;

while in his *Fourth Letter to a Young Poet* he strikes with clarity a sane middle note. 'Bodily delight', he writes, 'is a sense experience, just like pure seeing or the pure feeling with which a lovely fruit fills the tongue; it is a great boundless experience which is given us, a knowing of the world, the fullness and splendour of all knowing. Our acceptance of it is not bad; what is bad is that almost all men misuse and squander this experience, and apply it as a stimulus to the weary places of their lives, a dissipation instead of a rallying for the heights.'

It is clear, too, from the following, that Rilke deeply understood the profound relation of sex and song, the source of the lyrical in the erotic; the fact that however hidden it may be our life is irrigated by this physical spring. 'The thought of being a creator, of begetting and forming', he says, 'is nothing without its continual great confirmation and realization in the world, nothing without the thousand-fold assent from things and animals—and its enjoyment is so indescribably beautiful and rich only because it is full of inherited memories of the begetting and bearing of millions. In one creator's thought a thousand and forgotten nights of love revive again and fill it full of loftiness and grandeur. Those who come together in the nighttime and entwine in swaying delight perform a serious work and gather up sweetness, depth and strength for the song of some poet that is to be, who will rise to tell of unspeakable bliss.' Here, we may notice the de-carnalising touch, and how the description would better fit the nuptials of a tree and a hamadryad than the grosser mating of man and woman. Rilke, for all his pagan 'Yea-saying', had not a Dionysian mind. His temperament was Apollonian; and what interested him in Orpheus was not his awful loss but his potent song. He saw the phallus only as a peg for the lyre.

If, indeed, he foresaw without reference to Freud the sexual nature of the subconscious and its sublimation in art, he was no worshipper of Lawrence's 'dark gods'. For him, they represented chaotic forces, instincts to be tutored by the 'will for form'. This pre-social undergrowth of the *id* by means of which the child reaches back to the primitive past is described by the poet in his *Third Elegy*:

'... How he gave himself up to it! Loved.
Loved his interior world, his interior jungle,
that primal forest within, on whose mute overthrowness,
green-lit, his heart stood. Loved. Left it, continued
into his own roots and out into violent beginnings
where his tiny birth was already outlived. Descended,
lovingly, into the older blood, the ravines
where Frightfulness lurked, still gorged with his
    fathers.
    And every
terror knew him, and winked, and quite understood.'

Such, says Rilke, are the elements quickened by contact of
the male with woman; whose task is to use her civilising
touch (what Rémy de Gourmont and Coleridge call her
'conservative genius' and 'continuating' sense, respectively)
to mitigate and channelise these wild feelings:

'... —you have conjured up
prehistoric time in your lover. What feelings
whelmed up from beings gone by! What women
hated you in him! What sinister men
you roused in his youthful veins! Dead children
were trying to reach you . . . Oh, gently, gently
show him daily a loving, confident task done—guide him
close to the garden, give him those counter-
balancing nights . . .
                    Withhold him . . .'

Men, maintained Rilke, were careless 'botchers' of love;
and while the sentiments of the Elegy form an excellent
antidote against the modern mystique of lust, disseminated
by Hollywood and all those best-seller and purple-jacket
scribes who swallowed *Lady Chatterly's Lover* without an
attempt at mastication, the conclusion or remedy is open to
doubt. Why, after all, should woman be exempt from those
same chaotic dregs, that primitive residue decried in man?

The reasons for Rilke's belief in this are tortuous and not
easily come at. To begin with, Rilke despised and hated all
those characteristics of man known as exclusively masculine.
Perhaps, too, at the Military Academy, where he had spent
his boyhood years, and where he had been continuously
unhappy, he had likewise learnt to fear and avoid them. In his

15

Third Letter to a Young Poet he criticised Richard Dehmel—
that swashbuckling Bacchus of late nineteenth century German poetry—with a kind of restrained antipathy. There was,
he observed, in the spirit of his work 'no entirely mature and
unmixed sex world, but one which is not human enough,
merely masculine, which is heat, intoxication, and restless-
ness, and loaded with the old prejudices and arrogances with
which men have disfigured and burdened love'. So he dis-
poses of that Junker of song! Another factor in Rilke's
preference was probably the low estimate in which he held
the intellect and logic—qualities almost limited to man.
Opposed to these he posited female intuition, and the more
biological and organic and less mechanical methods of
thought; and he speaks of the 'innermost consciousness',
behind which 'the understanding' lags in a wondering out-
paced fashion. Finally, it is possible, that the breaking of his
own marriage with the sculptress Clara Westhoff, after only
a six months' trial—so avoiding the responsibility of a
domestic and paternal existence—might have produced a
sense of guilt from which he found an escape or release in
his generous but far-fetched assessment of woman.

From sex to love is one step, from love to marriage
another. Without accepting the common ideas regarding
these states, Rilke embraced them and found a place for
them in his scheme. As a personal living proposition, he
soon came to discard the second; but before the experiment
had proved a failure he set down his notions of it in a letter.
'I hold this to be the highest task', he wrote, 'for a union of
two people: that one shall guard the other's solitude.' Again,
in writing to the 'Young Poet' of the Letters, he speaks of
those couples who have not kept this law of respecting a
mutual privacy. The penalty they pay is to lose the expanses
and possibilities of communion for 'a sterile helplessness out
of which nothing more can come; nothing but a little disgust, disillusionment and poverty and deliverance into one
of the many conventions which are set up in large numbers
as public refuges along this most dangerous of roads.'

Before this sense of marital constriction, in his own case,
became too intense Rilke made his getaway; and little by
little there came to be formed the idea of 'love without the
beloved'. So, in his poem *The Risen One*, as C. M. Bowra has

16

pointed out, 'Rilke sees the Magdalene as one whom the Crucifixion makes to love Christ without wishing to be loved in return', and after the Resurrection the poet describes her new state of mind:

'She only comprehended later, hidden
Within her cave, how, fortified by death,
The gratefulness of oil he had forbidden
And the presentiment of touch and breath,

Meaning to form from her the lover
Who hangs no more on a beloved's choice,
Since, yielding to enormous storms above her,
She mounts in ecstasy beyond his voice.'

On just such a transcendentally dizzy note does the unknown young confessor (the author himself), in Kierkegaard's book *Repetition*, close the last letter to his confidant, on hearing of the marriage of his (the former's) ex-fiancée: 'The chalice of inebriation is again held out to me, already I inhale its fragrance, already I am sensible of its foaming music—but first a libation to her who saved a soul which sat in the solitude of despair. Hail to feminine magnanimity! Long life to the high flight of thought, to moral danger in the service of the idea! Hail to the danger of battle! Hail to the solemn exultation of victory! Hail to the dance in the vortex of the infinite! Hail to the breaking wave which covers me in the abyss! Hail to the breaking wave which hurls me up above the stars!'

As the confidant says of his correspondent's passion: 'The young girl was not his love, she was the occasion of awakening the primitive poetic talent within him and making him a poet. Therefore he could only love her, could never forget her, never wish to love anyone else; . . . She had meant much to him, she had made him a poet, and thereby she had signed her own death warrant.'

Love, then, as Rilke sees it, is a kind of rocket-platform, from whence—by the fuel of unrequited passion—one soars beyond the boundaries of narrow desire; a type of spiritual catapult-act. This amorous self-denial in the name of inspiration (self-denial sprung from creative accident) finds its expression in much of Rilke's writing, especially in *The*

Notebook of Malte Laurids Brigge. 'It would be difficult', he writes at the end, 'to persuade me that the story of the Prodigal Son is not the legend of one who did not want to be loved', and imagines this character thinking of 'the troubadours who feared nothing more than to be granted what they asked'. Significantly the book concludes: 'He was now terribly difficult to love, and he felt that One alone was capable of loving him. But He was not yet willing.'

This penultimate quotation is a reference to the rules of the Courts of Love in old Provençe, influenced, as Denis de Rougemont has observed, by the Albigensian heresy. Briefly, this rule in question stipulated that the troubadour should praise and adore his lady but never think to possess her person (she was generally married to another). The main contention of de Rougemont is, however, that woman—the beloved—was viewed by these gnostics as the direct gateway to God (short-cutting mediation by the Catholic Church). Access, then was believed possible between the troubadour and Hagia Sophia (the great vision of divine wisdom) only providing the lines of communication—i.e. the beloved woman—were kept free of all carnal traffic.

The resemblance between the Manichean (whose theories had affected the Albigensian Church, and who looked on procreation as a sin—Arnaut Daniel, one of the greatest troubadours, being himself a homosexual though he still made devotional songs to his lady) and the artist whose ultimate mistress is art is seen to be a powerful one. Both of them use women as an occasion; for both of them love is a kind of transformer, adapting the lower currents of passion to the higher currents of God or art. Neither view love as a social force, as something that generates and raises families, as something that prolongs and conserves society. The concepts of both of them are specialised and private; alien and remote from the life of everyday.

Perhaps, at this point, one may object that this constant reference to the needs of Everyman as a touchstone to judge the values discovered in a work of art is inapposite; that the greater minds of artist and thinker always sail beyond the requirements of the masses. Here we must make a clear distinction. It is evident that the artist's life must be seen in terms of the value of his art, and that we do not demand from him obedience to the by-laws of social convention if they should prove constrictive to his work—always providing that work in the end is seen to enrich our understanding with values that answer to our deepest needs. In other words, we may judge an author for his ability to provide us with functional answers to our needs: functional, that is, at a high imaginative level; long-range, long-term answers, so to speak.

Now, with regard to the question of love, this is a matter where Rilke fails us; and if it be said that his spirit was too great to descend to the actual business of living—the immediate problem addressed to us all of how to love in the tangible flesh—one has only to turn to such a thinker and such a poet as Solovyev and Shakespeare to see the question successfully approached in terms of the widest relevance. 'The purpose of love', wrote the former, 'is to vindicate and deliver individuality by destroying egoism'; and in order to ensure the continuance of this process the lover and beloved must stay together, enduring this purifying discipline of delight. 'Each single individual', he wrote in *The Justification of the Good*, 'possesses the potentiality of perfection, but by remaining isolated and limited an individual deprives himself of the real fullness of life, i.e. of perfection and infinity.'

Referring to Shakespeare, we here discover, worked out in his last plays (presumably, therefore, his late maturest feelings), what Middleton Murry calls a picture of the ideal normality of love. It would seem that in spite of the cruel experiences that Shakespeare knew and wrote of in the Sonnets (and possibly in *Troilus and Cressida*, *All's well that ends well*, and *Measure for Measure*) he retained a belief in love at first sight and marriage as its general best preservative; and it may well be that *The Tempest* contains the most exquisitely tempered optimism, the longest-tried time-proof smile of the mind anywhere to be found in the field of art and letters.

In his book *Passion and Society* de Rougemont remarks on the close relationship between the idea of mystical passion-love and death, and in his chapter on German Romanticism (which he describes as a 'new Albigensian heresy') he quotes Novalis to illustrate this sentiment. 'Our vows were not exchanged for this world' the poet remarks in his private diary on the death of his bride-to-be, while in his maxims he observes 'All passions end in tragedy. Whatever is finite ends in death. All poetry has a tragic element in it.'

True to this lineage of subjective German thinkers, Rilke, too, makes a cult of death. With him, however, we find modifications upon the original Manichean concept. Unlike earlier Romanticists, Rilke established no hard and fast division between the worlds of life and death. He constantly talked of the poet's task of keeping 'life open towards death', and regarded himself as dwelling in a kind of twin kingdom —this 'now first whole, first hale world' (as he calls it in his *Journal*).

In his earlier verse this idea of death has too often seemed to lend itself to the sentimental mitigation of a dark mystery. There is something precociously make-believe about it; a highly imaginative make-believe, but compensation-thinking none the less; and, what is more, a little dishonest. So, in his poem *The Death of the Beloved*, it appears that the poet is determined to discover some means or other to mitigate the grief. If not to be discovered, why, then he will invent!

'He only knew of death what all men may:
   that those it takes it thrusts into dumb night.
When she, however—no, not snatched away,
   but tenderly unloosened from his sight,

had glided over to the unknown shades,
   and when he felt that he had now resigned
the moonlight of her laughter to their glades,
   and all her ways of being kind:

then all at once he came to understand
   the dead through her, and joined them in her walk,
kin to them all; he let the others talk,
and paid no heed to them, and called that land
   the fortunately-placed, the ever-sweet.—
And groped out all its pathways for her feet.'

If Henry King could write in his famous *Exequy*:

'Wait for me there: I will not fail
   To meet thee in that narrow Vale.'

he at least was not playing the ostrich with death but speaking out of his deepest convictions, from a Christian and not a 'private only' approach. This suggestion of a compensating after-thought as being the starting-point of the poem is further strengthened by two factors. Firstly, Rilke's conception of God was one which depended on man's pre-existence. God, he believed, was 'built' by man; built daily by the artists, thinkers and saints—a Gothic cathedral of the ideal which every century enrichened and transformed. God was therefore co-extential with man: an attitude little lending itself to a ready belief in an after-life. The second of these factors—by far the most important—was the fear and pity Rilke felt at any occurrence of death. (The great *Requiem*, written on the decease of the painter Paula Mendersohn-Becker, confirms this remark through its deep pathos—more unflinchingly expressed there than in any other of his poems.) Long after his mourner's sugar-candy verses for *The Death of the Beloved*, he wrote in a letter to a friend: 'How is it possible to live, when the very elements of this life are completely incomprehensible to us? When continually we are inadequate in loving, uncertain in resolution, and incapable of facing death, how is it possible to exist?' Hardly the attitude of one much sheltered by the roof-tree of his fantasy!

True enough, in the magnificent *Tenth Elegy* a more durable conception of death appears. But again, its main interest is for the artist. Death is seen as the sphere of permanence; a realm of objects, perfected in form and proof against the depredations of time; a kind of 'Grecian Urn' universe; a metaphysical museum-world for Parnassian minds. In all, allowing for the discount occasioned by his earlier post-mortem Cockaigne, it seems that Rilke contributed less to a widely valid poetic eschatology than such a writer as Wordsworth, say, who offered us the consolation of a sort of stoical pantheism (*v*. his lovely lyric in the *Lucy* sequence 'A slumber did my spirit seal').

If Rilke's detached asocial nature left him at a disadvantage when he conceived his myths of love (holding him back from the creation of some universal image applicable to all, instead of seeing it as an elixir, rich in proteins for the artist and saint), it helped him to avoid several cliché-approaches when he came to write of the Hero. Especially was he fortunate in viewing the hero in non-racial terms—as a kind of national Hercules—in a country where Bismarck and the two Prussian Fredericks had tended to militarise the Fire-stealer myth, shadowing forth Prometheus in the dress of Grenadier.

Here, again, it would appear that Rilke, 'uncertain in resolution' (as he confessed himself to be), was bent on appeasing his own hesitation by the image of a figure 'immovably centred'. As this figure of the hero represents the ideal self of the poet there is no question of seeing it shown in the light of patriot or communal martyr. Rilke was always an individualist; and so he portrays the hero as seeking, not to shoulder the burdens of others—to discharge in himself the duties of the group—but rather to follow and achieve those quests peculiarly intended by fate for him alone. Thus we have the picture of hero as Independent: a being of internal integrity whose life is consummated in outward deeds.

'Ah, then', cries the poet as he hears the wind speaking to him of the hero's feats,

> '. . . How gladly I'd hide from the longing: Oh would,
> would that I were a boy, and might come to it yet, and
> be sitting,
> propped upon arms still to be, and reading of Samson,
> how his mother at first bore nothing, and, afterwards
> all.'

If in these lines we recognise the somewhat ingenuous yearning of a frustrated actionist with his nostalgia for more than verbal adventure, at least, we, who wriggle impotently in a universe full of collective Pop-eyes, national Al Capones, and mass-production scape-goats, are spared the embarrassment of seeing them in verse.

Action, says the poet, in some lovely lines of his splendid but still somewhat barren *Sixth Elegy*, is life's fruition; and its point of ripeness, death. So we are left perhaps a little incredulous—or depressed—regarding the hero's labours. What has all this epical pother been about? Who is this already half-transformed mortal, hunting his quest as a squire hunts a fox? And what is the point of human society, stepping in the foot-prints the hero has left in the spots that were plotted by an unspeaking fate? Possessed as he was of

22

a sense of the past, but with little sense of history—of man's continuation—the poet seems to leave these questions in the air.

If we were pleased to see Rilke eschewing a portrait of the hero as mass-saviour, we are the more surprised and sorry to find him reflecting the mass-hysteria of war. Yet this is just what we discover in the first two of the *Five Songs* written in August 1914. In *Song I* he raises popular excitement to the height of the panoplied figure of Mars. 'A god at last', he writes.

> '. . . Since the God of Peace so often
> eluded our grasp, the God of Battles has grasped us.'

This, of course, was the typical reaction which poets all over Europe expressed. Our own Rupert Brook excelled in it (producing the kind of poetry which might, one feels, well have its roots in a Decadent's late reading of *Henry V*). Just this crude school-boy volte-face from 'the lilies and languours of vice' to khaki and cannon-fodder enthusiasm was something unlooked for in the sensitive Rilke. For such a writer as the Hungarian Ady, diseased and surfeited with the pleasures of life, it was easy to imagine the carnage of war as a kind of purifying cure. 'Blood, blood, blood', the poet could write,

> 'Man will be much more beautiful
> once he is cleansed with blood,
> and better too.'

Apart from its therapeutic value, war for such a jaded rake would be the ultimate global *frisson*, a kind of final cosmic debauch.

In the case of Rilke's own acclamation none of these factors were operative. Even so, in the *Second Song* he goes one better, rivalling Wagner, and we hear the old Teutonic trombone once more desecrating the linden trees:

> '. . . O mothers, the joy of giving!
> Give as though you were infinite! Give! Be a
> bountiful Nature
> to these good-growing days. Send out your sons
> with a blessing.

> And girls, to think that they love you! To think
>   of being felt
>   in such hearts.'

As if this is not already bad enough, we have in addition that unfortunate piece of typical civilian flag-wagging in verse, *Now it is you I praise, Banner*.

Already, however, by the *Third Song* jubilation is exchanged for penitential grief, which does not altogether cover up a doubt. Pain, not anger, now maintains the poet-sacrifice and not fulfilment—these are the only goodnesses of war.

By the October of 1915, this dark half-mood of doubt had changed to one of frienzied protestation—a type of hysteria, in every way as extreme and unreal as his earlier outburst had been. 'Can no one hinder and stop it?' he wrote in a letter to a friend. 'Why is it that there are not two, three, five, ten persons gathered together in the market-place and shouting: "Enough!?" They would be shot down; but at least they would have given their lives to end the war; whereas those at the front are dying so that the horror shall go on and on.'

In another letter he wrote these self-revealing lines, loaded with a kind of hermetic egoism: '. . . I find it very hard to attain the valid, where possible, the somewhat fruitful, attitude to this monstrous universality. Happy are those that are within it, whom it carries away, whose voices it drowns!' The logic of this clumsy implication being, that the poet feels his own disturbance is of more consequence than another's loss of life.

In all these reactions, as C. M. Bowra points out, reality was testing the doctrines of Rilke: testing their durability; seeking out the poet's weakest links. 'O tell us, poet, what you do', he wrote—in the verses which J. B. Leishman calls 'an epitome of Rilke's *Religio Poetae*'—and unwaveringly back comes the answer 'I praise':

> 'But those dark, deadly, devastating ways,
>   how do you bear them, suffer them?—I praise.'

And later, this faculty for total celebration is taken as proof of the poet's credentials:

'And whence your right in every kind of maze,
in every mask, to remain true—I praise.'

Just this elaborate æsthetic façade it has taken two wars
to reveal in its weakness. The point is that one cannot
always praise. One must then denounce or learn to be dumb,
or turn to praise that to which value still adheres. This was
never understood by Rilke, whose power to bless was only
matched by his lack of a power to truly assess. The most
difficult task of the poet, namely, the retention of praise
with values was something he did not constantly effect. The
first distinction he certainly achieved: he won to that conscious pinnacle from whose tip the spirit is aware of all
things, looking reality squarely in the face. This is the state
of understanding or acceptance: the realisation that such
things are. The second step, however, of acclamation; of
celebrating all things possessed of value, and denouncing or
ignoring those things without it, was one which Rilke failed
to make. He did not comprehend that acclamation must be
preceded by selection; that the poet must sift the things of
the world just as he sorts and sifts his words.

Perhaps the factor at the root of this instability of judgment in Rilke was his dependence on sensitivity: his passive
over-readiness in the reception of phenomena. 'All absolute
sensation', said Novalis, 'is religious'; so helping us to see
how the transcendental æstheticism of Rilke was prone to
fall a victim to the powerful impact of events. 'Oh to see
men in the grip of something', the poet exalts in his *Second
Song*. 'Whatever it is?' one feels like adding. A case of
intensity at all costs!

Another recurrent element in the poet's change of heart
with regard to war was the dictation of a purely personal
need. For some months Rilke was obliged to act in a clerical
capacity, far behind the lines, in Army dress. This, much
more than external horror, clarified and strengthened his
growing disenchantment. 'Never', he wrote in 1919, 'have
I been so far beyond the reach of the wind in the spaces, of
the trees, of the stars by night. Ever since I had to stare out
at all this from the evil disguise of an infantry uniform, it
has been alienated from me . . .' He, who had so affirmed the
individual, was learning the grief of being anonymous.

Love, death, war (and their sum-total, life): these are the themes of the major poets, and Rilke's responses to them have been shown. In each case we see how his attitude seems to have been compulsorily dictated by the needs and claims of his artistic life. In the name of the poet he sacrificed the man, and on art's high altar he gave himself and others. Here, it would appear he lacked that double hunger which animated the greatest poets: the twin adoration of poetry and life. So it arises that in his work we look in vain for the full-blooded zest, the thronging reflections of jostling beings, that ant-hill movement of living colours.

This absence, however, is a modern trait. We find it harder to be jolly and kind than Homer, Chaucer, or Shakespeare did. Added to this contemporary 'Angst'—this lack of elation about existence—a further defect must be advanced. Rilke had hardly any interest, any affection for the grown-up world. Adult human life meant little to him. As his friend, the philosopher Kassner wrote: 'In truth he had not this masculine separation between judgment and feeling that belongs so peculiarly to man. Oh, he took absolutely no cognizance of man. Man remained an intruder in Rilke's world; only children, women, and old people were at home in it.'

Locked in his 'separate fantasy' more exclusively than most great artists, he failed as a modern mythologist because —as he said—he skipped the human. (One cannot, after all, find a full-scale mythos in a system of animals, Angels, and things.)

Rilke's mythology is limited, then; and only significant for the few. It is not so broad as that of Hölderlin or de Nerval, or—in our own times—that of T. S. Eliot, though, perhaps, it is deeper than two of these three. (Here it seems relevant to remark that the poetic mythology of a whole generation was that of 'The Wasteland'—a negative one. Since the poet has reached a more positive position in the climate of 'The Four Quartets' his mythology has lost its popular appeal.—'Everyman' is still in the spiritual desert. It is now the mythology of the solitary mystic; alone, even, in the presence of his Church and the wide Communion of the Saints.)

Just as Eliot interprets man to man only so far as the individual inclines to be a religious solitary like himself, so

26

Rilke explains man to man in so far as he inclines to be a poet. His is an artist's mythology for artists.

Once this limitation has been understood, the treasure which his poetry offers is enormous. It is true that we miss the bovine exultation of such a poet as Apollinaire, the salty immediacy of Lorca, the athletic conjuring of Boris Pasternak. Compared with these poets there is, indeed, something of a glorified old maid about him, a kind of exquisite far-flung Platonic shimmer, a rarefied thirst to penetrate the sky.

This, in its own way, of course, is his attraction; a quality reserved exclusively for him. Rilke discovered a new use for the earth; a fresh justification for existence. This was, to furnish the poet's spiritual landscape, which in turn would be the landscape of an earthly future. Here, no phenomena must be omitted; and again and again Rilke took on trust the entire gamut of destructive elements, achieving sometimes those rare poems where the Janus nature of existence is seen like a shield whose one side displays putrefaction while the other is bright as a peacock's tail.

Never was there any question with Rilke of settling down comfortably with his vision; of putting things ship-shape once and for all. Persistently he felt the need to liberate the clothed heart's Holy Ghost; and in such poems as *The Harrowing of Hell* we find him adventuring on the farthest fringe of thought—that stratospherical frontier-land, dizzy with the threat of infinite space. To read these verses is like a revelation of beacons, statues, towers, and proclamations seen and heard on the out-posts of the mind. No other poet conveys like him the feel of the vistas of psychic distance.

Another great quality peculiar to Rilke is the way in which his poetry looks ahead. For him, the sensibility is continually unlocking the doors of the future. He never allows his dæmon to grow fat.

More, too, than any other poet Rilke accomplished the difficult task of painting intangibilities; of describing silence, water, wind, and air. Read, for example, the following poems: *Shatter me, music*; *Soul in Space*; *What stillness round a God*; and the verses to *Night*—sympathetic hand-shakes of the mind with pure dimension.

One might, perhaps, hazard a comparison of Rilke with that poet of contemporary physics—James Jeans.

27

Roland Gant

ARTURO BAREA
A WRITER OF THE PEOPLE

A Study of
The Forge, The Track, and *The Clash*

ROM the end of the 1914–1918 war until 1936 Spain and her affairs were very much in the background of the European scene. Shut away behind the Pyrenees, Spain, for English people, was the country which produced nuts and oranges for the children at Christmas, the place where British money and enterprise developed the mineral wealth for the benefit of Britain and the world. This isolation was not lessened by Spanish neutrality in the first World War and to most English children growing up between the wars the knowledge of Spain was confined to the Armada, Don Quixote, and the burial of Sir John Moore. Of modern Spain, her internal politics and her people, little was known and it was felt that she could have little influence on contemporary history. Like Greece, she was a country with a glorious past and an unimportant and nondescript present occasionally enlivened by changes of government and *coups d'état*.

So, in the middle 'thirties, while all eyes in France and Britain were turned towards the methodical railway-time-table advance of Mussolini's new Roman Empire and the ascendancy of Hitler at the head of the armed and singing youth of Germany, the Spanish Republic which had replaced the monarchy in 1931 faced a growing crisis. As the result of an amnesty granted to such Catholic Fascists as Calvo Sotelo and the fostering by the Church and the officer caste of all anti-Republican movements, the Spanish Republic in 1936 found itself menaced by four powerful Right-Wing groups.

28

These were the Falange Española of José Antonio Primo de Rivera, a Catholic Party under the leadership of Gil Robles, another Catholic-Fascist group under Calvo Sotelo, and a general Right-Wing reactionary group under two generals —Mola and Sanjurjo. This intrigue and regrouping of the Right for an assault upon the Republic aroused little comment in the outside world—apart from Italy and Germany where advice and promises of support were given to the potential rebels.

When the revolt began, opinion was sharply divided in France and England. In Britain demonstrations and meetings were arranged by the Left in support of the Republic while the Conservative Press concentrated on representing the rebels as the 'Nationalists' who were fighting anti-Christ, Bolshevism, Moscow gold, and all the other bogeys which haunt the reactionaries of every country. Spain was on the map again as the focus of the eyes of the world. The bid for power by Fascism had come to Europe in the form of open warfare and the struggle was carried vicariously into every party office and meeting-place of Europe. Spain became a symbol.

This brings me to the point of this preamble—Spain the symbol. I have sketched very roughly the position of Spain in Europe during the period preceding the Civil War and the parties of the Right who precipitated it. The subsequent history is known to all—the armed intervention of Italy and Germany on behalf of the rebels, the unofficial aid given to the Government by the Soviet Union and France, the formation of the International Brigades and the non-intervention policies of the Western Powers which lost them the first round in the battle against Fascist-National Socialist world conquest. Both sides were vociferous in their claims of fighting for the 'liberation of the Spanish people' but even at the end of the war very few English or French people knew anything about the common people of Spain whose destiny was being decided. One hears of the various leaders, of popular figures in this or that party, but what is known of Juan Perez, the Bill Smith and John Doe of Spain? What was the life of the working-class Spaniards during the years which led the plotting of a revolution, the war itself, and the taking of Spain as a symbol?

Out of that final conflict emerged a writer who speaks for the common Spaniard. Although the epithet 'a working-class writer' has been abused in its use I do not hesitate to apply it to Arturo Barea. In addition to speaking for the Spaniard, Barea speaks for the international working class, and the value of what he says is increased tremendously by his ability to tell the story of his life without being influenced by subsequent events and later conclusions. When one reads of his childhood and youth, one sees the people and places as he saw them at that time. His three volumes of autobiography, *The Forge*, *The Track*, and *The Clash*, are not propagandist but comprise the story in which the author happens to be a figure seen objectively.

The Forge tells the story of Arturo Barea's childhood in Madrid as the son of a poor widow who earned her living by washing clothes. It begins:

'The wind blew into the two hundred pairs of breeches and filled them. To me they looked like fat men without a head, swinging from the clothes-lines of the drying-yard. We boys ran along the rows of white trousers and slapped their bulging seats. Señora Encama was furious. . . .'

He writes of his mother:

'My mother is stroking my head, my tousled hair, my unruly cowlick, and her fingers pass idly over my head, but I feel them inside me. When her hand lies still I take it and look at it. So very tiny, so thin, worn by the water of the river, with small tapering fingers, the fingertips pricked by the lye, with twisted blue veins, nervous and alive. Alive with warmth and blood, alive in quick motion, always ready to leap and fly, to scrub vigorously, to stroke gently. I love to press them to my cheeks and rub my skin against them, to kiss and nibble her fingertips . . . .'

Later, writing again of his mother, he captured completely the helplessness of the poor with a simplicity that is more moving than fury:

'I was a man. I had my standing. Employee of the Credit Etranger. My mother worked down by the river. She must stop working there. I didn't want to watch her any more climbing the stairs on Mondays and Tuesdays and saying: "Run down and fetch the milk, will you, I'm tired." I didn't want any more to smell the dirty linen piling up in our room during the week, with its sour smell like mouldy wine. I didn't want any more to see Señor Manuel leaning heavily against the walls by the garret door, with sweat bubbles on his forehead after the climb, easing down a six-foot stack of washing, gently, so that the bundle should not burst. I didn't want any more to count the sheets and the pants of Señor So-and-so and to make out the bills.

'I didn't want to accompany her any more in the evenings, to deliver the bundles of clean linen and collect the dirty washing, and to wait in the house-doors for her to come down and say: "They didn't pay me." When she came back to our street, my mother went to the baker. "Juanito, please, give me a loaf . . . I'll pay you tomorrow." Then to the grocer. "Antonio, give me four pounds of potatoes and half a pound of dried cod . . . I'll pay you tomorrow." And so we had our supper. The gentle-folk didn't pay her for washing their sweaty, mucky pants with buttons missing, and therefore the washerwoman couldn't pay for her supper. My mother was pleased because the tradesmen trusted her, I was furious because she had to beg favours and because the nobs hadn't paid her. But I ate my supper. My mother was so glad that I had something for supper although the gentle-folk hadn't paid her, that I had to eat it.'

In Spain, as all over the world, poverty is a crime, the poor a blemish on the face of the earth, to be spurned and hounded from the places where they may offend the eyes of the wealthy and respectable. Here is one account:

'When the poor people had to go in ragged clothes and one saw their naked skin, just because they had nothing else to wear, they were not allowed into church to pray, and if they insisted the police were fetched and detained them. But the big chests in the sacristy were filled with good clothes and jewels for the Saints, and the wooden images were clothed and decked with diamonds and velvet. Then all the priests would come out, just as in the Royal Theatre, in silver and golden robes, while the candles were lit and the organ played and the choir sang; and during the singing the sacristans would pass round the collection boxes. When everything was over they locked up the church and the poor people stayed under the porch to sleep in their nakedness. Inside was the Virgin, still in her golden crown and velvet

31

mantle, very snug and warm, because the church was carpeted and the stoves burning. The Child Jesus was dressed in gold-embroidered little pants and he also had a velvet cloak and crown of diamonds. Under the porch was a poor woman for whom my mother had once bought ten centimos' worth of hot milk because she showed us her wrinkled, dried-up breasts, while her baby was crying, half-naked. She sat in the porch of the church of Santiago, on a litter of waste paper, and said to my mother: "May God reward you, my dear".'

The Forge is full of living characters, both of Madrid and Castile, Grandmother Ines, Uncle Hilario, Uncle Luis, the Basque priest Father Joaquin, and the many others amongst whom the boy learned the complex pain and sweetness of living.

The second volume of the trilogy, *The Track*, deals with the period of the author's military service in Morocco. Whilst retaining his power of keen and sensitive observation Barea writes with very little of the gentleness and lyrical description which characterises *The Forge*. This time he writes, not through the eyes of a child, but of a young man shocked into awareness of the corruption, waste, and intrigue in which were embedded the roots of the tragedy to come. Again he succeeds in speaking for all of us. As a Spanish soldier with the problems peculiar to the army of his country he nevertheless speaks for every soldier conscripted from the working class. He says in a foreword to the book:

'A very distinguished critic of *The Forge* pointed out that "the experiences chronicled by the author" are not "at all singular", and that "the conversations . . . the discoveries . . . and the disillusionments of experience are such as could be described by millions . . .". This is perfectly true of the present book too, and is as I think it should be. (It is, incidentally, also the reason why I cannot consider these books as straight autobiographies.) The millions who shared the same experiences and disappointments do not usually write, but it is they who are the rank and file in wars, revolutions, and "New Orders", they who carry on in the Old Order, helpless, restless, and disillusioned. Some of them defended Madrid, some evacuated Dunkirk; others died for General Franco; some of them in this country wonder just what the war is about. They are usually called the common people or the "little men" or the "lower orders". As I was one of them, I have attempted to be vocal on their behalf, not in the form of propaganda, but simply by giving my own truth.'

During his service in Morocco he came into contact with Spanish officers who were later to take part in the rebellion. It is in writing of them that Barea displays his artistry in viewing his own life with an objective detachment. Instead of succumbing to the temptation to write of the generals in the light of their later actions he depicts them as they appeared to him at the time. For instance, when he writes of Millán Astray the effect he produces in showing a proud, brutal, and fanatically brave soldier who could compel men to follow him to hell if necessary, is far more revealing than if he were to write consciously of him as one who was to become a leader in the army of Franco. Here is a description of Millán Astray addressing his men on the eve of a battle:

' "Gentlemen of the Legion . . . yes, gentlemen. Gentlemen of the Tercio of Spain," he began, and ended "You have come here to die. It is to die that one joins the Legion . . . the Betrothed of Death. Long live Death!"

'Millán Astray's whole body underwent an hysterical transfiguration. His voice thundered and sobbed and shrieked. Into the faces of these men he spat all their misery, their shame, their ugliness, their crimes, and then he swept them along in fanatical fury to a feeling of chivalry, to a readiness to renounce all hope, beyond that of dying a death which would wash away their stains of cowardice in the splendour of courage.

'When the Standard shouted in wild enthusiasm, I shouted with them.

'Sanchiz pressed my arm:

' "He's a grand fellow, isn't he?"

'Millán Astray went round the circle of legionaries, stopping here or there before the most exotic or the most bestial faces. He stopped in front of a mulatto with thick lips, the liverish yellow-white of his rounded eyeballs shot with blood.

'"Where do you come from, my lad?"

'"What the devil's that to you?" the man answered.

'Millán Astray stared straight into the other's eyes.

'"You think you're brave, don't you? Listen. Here, I am the Chief. If anyone like you speaks to me he stands to attention and says: 'At your orders, sir. I don't want to say where I come from.' And that's as it should be. You've a perfect right not to name your country, but you have no right to speak to me as if I were the likes of you.'

'"And in what are you more than I am?" The man spat from lips wet with saliva as if they were on heat.

'At times men can roar. At times men can pounce as though their muscles were of rubber and their bones steel rods.

'"I . . ." roared the commander. "I am more than you, more of a man than you!" He sprang at the other and caught him by the shirt collar. He lifted him almost off the ground, hurled him into the centre of the circle and smacked his face horribly with both hands. It lasted two or three seconds. Then the mulatto recovered from the unexpected assault and jumped. They hit each other as men in the primeval forest must have done before the first stone axe was made. The mulatto was left on the ground nearly unconscious, bleeding.

'Millán Astray, more erect, more terrifying than ever, rigid with a furious homicidal madness, burst into the shout:

'"Attention!"

'The eight hundred legionaries—and I—snapped into it like automatons. The mulatto rose, scraping the earth with his hands and knees. He straightened himself. His nose poured blood mixed with dirt like a child's mucus. The torn lip was more bloated than ever. He brought his heels together and saluted. Millán Astray clapped him on his powerful back:

'"I need brave men at my side tomorrow. I suppose I'll see you near me."

'"At your orders, sir." Those eyes, more bloodshot than ever, more yellow with jaundice, held a fanatical flame.'

Like most sensitive and imaginative people, Barea suffered intensely from the sights of carnage he witnessed and he brings to his story an intensity which makes the descriptions

34

more imaginatively horrible than any I have ever read. He describes a house in Melilla which he entered after the massacre:

'In the ground-floor rooms bloody tracks, traces of men dragged away by the shoulder with blood streaming down their boots and tracing two wavering lines as of red chalk on the stone flags.

'And then the back room.

'A little boy has got hold of a jug of chocolate sauce in his mother's absence. He has painted his face and hands, his legs and his clothes, the table and the chair. He has climbed down from the chair and poured a big blob of chocolate on the floor. He has passed his fingers across the walls and left the print of his hand in every corner, on every piece of furniture, in lines, hooks and hieroglyphs. Jumping up and down in his joy at seeing dark stripes on all the clean things, he has put his feet in the jug and splashed the chocolate on the walls, right up high. It was so beautiful that he has plunged both hands into the jug and spattered big and little drops everywhere. Right in the middle a big blob has stuck half-dry.

'In the back room were five dead men. They were smeared with their own blood, face, hands, uniforms, hair, and boots. The blood had made pools on the floor, stripes on the walls, blobs on the ceiling, sprawling splashes in all the corners. On every clean, white place it had painted hands with five or two or one finger, fingerless palms and shapeless thumbs. A table and a few chairs were turned into scattered kindling-wood. Countless flies, droning incessantly, were sucking blood from the thumb printed on the wall and from the lips of the corpse in the left-hand corner. . . . The smell dissolved our human substance. It tainted it instantaneously and turned it into a viscous mass. To rub one's hands was to rub two hands which did not belong to one, which seemed to be those of a rotting corpse, sticky and impregnated with the smell.'

Some time after, Arturo Barea was on sick-leave in Madrid. His mother placed on his plate some steak and chips—'But since the dead of Melilla I could not touch meat. The sight and smell of it invariably made me see and smell corpses, rotting or burning on a petrol-soaked fire, and made me vomit. It produced an immediate mental association and reaction against which I was powerless. I wanted to master myself, and began cutting the meat on my plate. Rosy juice trickled out. I was sick.'

The Track is the link between the story of Barea the man and the events which culminated in the Spanish Civil War and the part played in it by Barea the Republican. He relates the tricks and rackets of the officers in Morocco by which they cheated Government, soldiers, and Moors alike in order to line their pockets and the misery of the lice-infested soldiers fed on mouldy beans flavoured with red pepper. He shows their helplessness as soldiers—and as civilians—before the power of the ruling caste.

With *The Clash* Arturo Barea attains the crescendo of his story and the way in which it became bound up with the story of Spain itself. In it everything of which he told in the two earlier books meets; his private life and problems, his faith as a Republican, and the final agony of Spain in the grip of the inevitable civil war and her new part as the European battle-ground of rival ideologies and power politics.

So much that has been written of the Spanish War has come from foreigners whose accounts have usually been biased by the part they took and the aspect they were determined upon seeing before they went. The journalists often wrote what they knew their papers wanted or that which their political consciences demanded. The International Brigadiers lived in their own world of ideals and had little contact with the ordinary Spanish people and they viewed the war in a very different way from those whose homes and families were directly involved.

Through Barea's book one sees the war as it appeared to a Spaniard who, although working actively for the Republican cause, was not so blinded by fanaticism that he could not see the faults of his own side. With the same objectivity with which he wrote of his early life in the first two books of the trilogy he tells of the internal jealousies and bitterness which split the ranks of the anti-Fascist forces. Above all he shows the suspicion and motives of personal or political party revenge which so frequently led to cruelty and injustice at a time when solidarity was needed. It often resulted in scenes similar to those of the Reign of Terror. Writing of

36

a member of one of the people's courts, a man nicknamed Little Paws, he says:

'The young Miliciano, Little Paws and a third taciturn man constituted themselves as a People's Tribunal, with Antonio as counsel for the defence. Two Milicianos brought in the first prisoner, a twenty-year-old boy, his elegant suit dirty with dust and cobwebs and his eyelids reddened.

' "Come nearer, my fine bird, we won't eat you," Little Paws jeered at him.

'The militiaman in the arm-chair took a list from the desk and read out the name and the details. The accused belonged to Falange; several comrades had seen him selling Fascist newspapers, and on two occasions he had taken part in street fights. When he was arrested, a lead cosh, a pistol, and a Falange membership card were found on him.

' "What have you got to say for yourself?" the judge in the chair asked.

' "Nothing. I've had bad luck." The prisoner fell back into a defiant silence, his head bent, his hands rubbing against each other. Little Paws leant forward from his chair:

' "All right. Take him away and bring the next one."

'When we were alone, the judge asked: "Are we all agreed?"

'The three of them and Antonio all answered in the affirmative; the Fascist would be taken out and shot that night.'

It was in Spain that the term 'Fifth Column' was first used,' by the Fascist besieging forces outside Madrid. It was an old idea with a new name, older than the Trojan Horse and based upon the very sound idea that distrust and suspicion is one of the most powerful demoralising agents and particularly when cultivated amongst those who are besieged or undergoing a temporary defeat. Anyone who was in England in 1940 will remember the Fifth Column scare, the stories of lights which shone when the Luftwaffe came, the strangers who talked to soldiers in pubs, and the wholesale internment of aliens.

Arturo Barea shows in *The Clash* how much more dangerous and far-reaching was this suspicion in Madrid during the siege. Then there were the added complications of the jealous rivalry between the various Spanish political factions and the misunderstandings between the groups of volunteers from other countries, the arrogance, (sometimes conscious, sometimes unconscious), of the foreign journalists and their attempts to get uncensored stories through to their papers. This distrust amongst people who were fighting in a common cause was fostered from without and irritated from within until it became an enemy which could strike down as suddenly as a bullet, swift and deadly and rendered more tragic because born of fear and sometimes mixed with personal jealousy and hatred. In Spain this distrust often hampered the progress of the war against Franco and hamstrung those who, like Barea himself, could see beyond the petty differences to the major issues. Even he did not escape suspicion and was hampered by it.

When the war began Arturo Barea trained clerks and office boys in the use of weapons and afterwards worked in the central telephone building as censor and broadcaster. His Moroccan experiences, and especially Melilla, had bitten deep into him. They came to the surface again with a violence which was to lead to his eventual nervous collapse. The images which lacerated his nerves and seared his imagination are described with a vividness and a detail which makes the reader feel, see, and remember them. There is, for example, the following account of an incident during the siege of Madrid which I think, once read, can never be forgotten:

'The street was filled with glaring sunlight and curls of slowly thinning smoke. Dull thuds sounded from further up Shell Alley. The porter informed me that our drivers were waiting round the corner in the Calle de la Montera, which was safer. I walked ahead of the women to find the cars. At the corner itself a gust of the familiar acrid smell hit me. Out of the corner of my eye I saw something odd and filmy sticking to the huge show-window of the Gramophone Company. I went close to see what it was. It was moving.

'A lump of grey mass, the size of a child's fist, was flattened out against the glass pane and kept twitching. Small, quivering drops of grey matter were spattered around it. A fine thread of watery blood was trickling down the pane, away from the grey-white lump with the tiny red veins, in which the torn nerves were still lashing out.

'I felt nothing but stupor. I looked at the scrap of man stuck on to the shop window and watched it moving like an automaton. Still alive. A scrap of human brain . . . . the shop window of the Gramophone Company, a display of black discs showing the white, cock-eared dog on their gaudy labels; the smooth pane reflecting the passing multitude, a phantom multitude of living beings without life; the black records enclosing in their furrows a multitude of ghost voices; everything unreal, and the only real thing above them—on the surface of that solid glass pane—a scrap of palpitating brain, still living, the antennæ of its severed nerves lashing out in a desperate voiceless cry to a deaf multitude.'

If I seem to emphasise the accounts of death in Barea's books it is because they illustrate so well the tortured pity which he has for suffering humanity, and it is this pity and the whole of human emotion which fills Barea. These human attributes, together with his origin as a man of the people in the truest sense, enable him through his imaginative and descriptive genius to speak for the common people of Spain. And, because of the strength and honesty of his writing, he speaks for the common people of the world. Those of us who belong to the working class know that the problems facing us and the experiences we undergo are identical in essence with those Spaniards whose youth was full of bitterness against the tyranny and exploitation by the ruling caste and the interests of big business, the power of a religious hierarchy, and the self-seeking chauvinism of the rich.

Before I end I must mention somebody who plays a very large part in Arturo Barea's life—his wife, Ilsa. Through the violence and suffering of the war related in *The Clash* there runs the thread of the love story of these two people. It is not a Hollywood-style story of two adolescents thrown into one another's arms against a background of burning cities and billowing smoke but of two mature people. Ilsa was an Austrian Socialist with a long and splendid record of organising the workers, imprisonment, and faith in the Left which had left her little time for her married life with an Austrian. Barea was married and had a family, was dissatisfied and only moderately content with a mistress.

When Ilsa first arrived in Madrid he was annoyed at having a woman to work with and he resented her efficiency and was amazed at her coolness. But during the siege and a short holiday together, through their mutual danger and their common beliefs they—perhaps inevitably, found that they were complementary to one another. When the final collapse came in Spain and the Fascists were making their final advance towards victory they left Spain together and went to France. The passages telling of their life together in Paris are some of the most touching in the book. The two refugees, of different nationality but of one belief—the belief which made refugees of them, living in great poverty in the France of that time, peaceful with an almost ominous quiet after Spain, turning her eyes away deliberately from the tragedy which was being played to a close in the neighbouring country. So it was that Arturo and Ilsa began their life together, cooking Spanish and Austrian dishes over a small stove in the hotel room where they lived or talking with the *restauratrice*, a discerning woman who recognised penniless lovers and perhaps realised that they were only the first victims of the many who would be engulfed in the rising tide of Fascism which was eventually to invade her own France and her very restaurant. She told them to eat there and pay when they had the money.

Seen superficially, the trilogy tells the story of the life of the little boy in Madrid, the youth in Africa, the Republican who lived through the first Fascist aggression and victory in Europe, and the man who solved the problem of his unsatisfactory and incomplete family life by entering into a relationship with a woman with whom he found love and understanding on the basis of a true equality. But there is much more in it than that. As I pointed out in the beginning of this article, the value of these three books lies in the universality of the writer's experience and his ability to see his life objectively and draw his conclusions and lessons from it. It is in this that the power and the value of Arturo Barea's writing lies. As a truly working-class writer he takes the ordinary events of his early life, his family and friends, and the events in which he took part and writes of them with an imagination and perception which renders him eloquent, not only for himself and his country, but for the millions like us among the common people of the world.

Books by Arturo Barea

The Forge (Faber)
The Track (Faber)
The Clash (Faber)
Lorca: the Poet and his People (Faber)
Struggle for the Spanish Soul. 1941. (Searchlight
Books: Secker and Warburg)
The above are translated into English by Ilsa Barea.

Montgomery Belgion

LYDGATE AND DOROTHEA

OUR LIVES are dramatic in that in appearance at least we must all constantly choose, and that our choices often turn out in retrospect to seem wrong. But the biography that does not go beyond a wrong choice and its consequences is elementary by the side of that in which one wrong choice commands later a second that is right.

It is a commonplace that our choices, be they wrong or right, are made amid traps and pitfalls. Many an actual life, it would seem, is a tale of days spent in pursuing that which the agent did not really want, and the substance was dropped for the shadow. A potentially brilliant actor, say, strives in vain to become an accomplished musician, neglecting the one talent he has in the effort to utilise a talent which never can be his. Or a wife imagines that it is in unfaithfulness that she obtains the contentment and satisfaction which are actually waiting for her all the time at her own fireside. Into this kind of error the imaginative writer is prone to fall in a way all his own. He may rightly identify himself to be in possession of the penman's gift and yet go astray in the use which he makes of it. Ben Jonson was some time in discovering that he could write comedies better than he could tragedies. His congenial style or form—novel, play, biography, essay—a writer may spoil many pages and spend many years in failing to discover. Or care and effort may be lavished on a novel in order to display characters in one light when it is in another that readers would see them as most moving and unforgettable.

In art as in life the problem is to know where the mistake lies. But for the illumination which may come upon us in the grief of a sudden bereavement or at the height of such an emotional crisis as may follow on the invasion of our country, it might perhaps seem as if this knowledge were never vouchsafed to us. In saying 'Know thyself' Socrates perhaps summed up all wisdom: there is no task more sisyphean. Sometimes, indeed, it is an outsider—the wise priest, the candid friend—whose insight, operating in detachment, can give us that fleeting glimpse of the hidden motives and real intentions that lie within us beyond the reach of our own penetration.

Middlemarch is generally recognised to be George Eliot's most ambitious novel. That it is also a striking artistic success English critics have not been as ready to affirm. Only the other day I saw it grudgingly conceded to be 'the greatest English novel of the nineteenth century'; but the tribute did not go the length of admitting it is a masterpiece. Unquestionably the whole of George Eliot's imaginative prose is marred by mannerisms of story-telling insufferable to numerous readers at the present time, and in this respect *Middlemarch* is no better than the rest. George Eliot, alas, is not a moralist but a moralizer, and her moralising is repellently sententious. Whatever obstacle the mannerisms may constitute, however, the theme is so compelling and worked out in such patient and vivid detail that even now the merits of the novel go on being experienced and acknowledged. But I do not believe that any English reader has ever yet in public done *Middlemarch* justice.

To account for this I have a suggestion. In a sense the novel is well-named. It is not really the story of the imaginary town of Middlemarch in the imaginary county of Loamshire. But it is crowded with characters and could not appropriately have taken its title from any one of them. Among these many characters, however, the nature of the reader's capacity to be interested requires that a few should stand in relief. These prominent characters have one thing in common. When we look back over the whole long novel once we have read it to the end, we notice that they are all married couples. In fact, *Middlemarch* is about marriage and married life.

Moreover, the number of characters does nothing to vitiate the novel's artistic integrity. It has a solid unity. At the same time as all the married couples become known to the reader in a lively intimacy, three of the marriages—those

43

of the Caleb Garths, the Bulstrodes, and the Vincys—mirror, so to speak, two others, and it is in these two that the dramatic quality of the story inheres. They are the marriages of Tertius Lydgate and Dorothea Brooke.

Lydgate is twenty-seven when in 1829 he buys and takes up a medical practice in the town of Middlemarch. He has studied in Paris under great men whose names still live. Their enthusiasm for medical advance has been contagious. Not only is he bent on adopting new methods of treatment; he means also to win celebrity, as Jenner has done, by the independent value of his researches. He intends to investigate the nature of fever, and, if possible, to discover a common principle of organic growth. But he is not well off. Once he has bought the practice, his capital amounts to no more than £800. If he is to crown his scientific ambitions, it is obvious that he must obey three rules. He will have to live modestly, win the allegiance of the largest possible number of private patients, and postpone all thought of marriage. Instead he quickly marries a dowerless girl, alienates possible patients, lives extravagantly, and gets heavily into debt. On top of all, he is innocently mixed up in a scandal. He is rescued—it might almost be said 'providentially'—from the pit of financial disgrace. But circumstances have by now defeated him. He decides to abandon all effort at research and to seek instead to be a fashionable physician in London. Oddly enough—for men with a flair for research are not always thought capable of adopting a money-making bedside manner—we are asked to accept that he succeeds.

Such, very superficially, is the history of the first of the two marriages that together form the substance of the novel *Middlemarch*. From the standpoint of success in research, Lydgate's crucial wrong choice is that which he makes in favour of a premature and improvident marriage. The other marriage, that of Dorothea Brooke, is intended by the novelist to appear equally misguided. Dorothea is an orphan who has grown up abroad. She is not yet twenty when she and her younger sister come to live with their bachelor uncle and guardian at Tipton Grange. She is as beautiful as the heroine of a novel should be. But her most important characteristic for the story is that she longs to give herself to some great cause. Village charities, patronage of the humbler clergy, the care of her soul over her embroidery in her own boudoir—from such contentment she is shut out The intensity of her religious disposition, the coercion which it exercises over her life, and a theoretic element in her ardent nature cause her in combination to struggle within the bands of the narrow education she has received and to give her a feeling of being hemmed in by a social life which seems to be nothing but a labyrinth of petty courses. She wants somehow to do good, although what good and how she should do it she does not know. To her the world and human nature are still a sealed book. The only visible way of escape from subjection to her own ignorance seems to be through union with a man older than herself and correspondingly wise who will impart his wisdom. She is ready to find that a husband can replace the father whom she has virtually never known.

A wealthy bachelor parson in the neighbourhood, Edward Casaubon, thirty years her senior, is thinking it is time he had an amanuensis and that the most docile would be one who was also a wife. He has a reputation for scholarship, resting vaguely on the report that he has been engaged for many years in the preparation of a weighty book. To Dorothea's inexperience he appears to be the very husband she fancies she needs. Nevertheless, in accepting him, she makes a choice more emphatically wrong than that which Lydgate makes. For Casaubon is constitutionally even less capable than Rosamond of coming up to expectation, and even more insatiably demanding. The honeymoon is spent in Rome, and notwithstanding his reputed erudition he proves too dull and desiccated to make the place vivid and interesting to Dorothea. She has expected to become his literary assistant, but he turns out to be reticent and suspicious with her about his work. From a young cousin of his, Will Ladislaw, she learns that he has been prevented by a neglect to learn German from keeping abreast of scholarship in his subject. When they have settled down at home, the young cousin reappears, and Casaubon grows unpleasantly jealous.

Presently, however, he dies, and although his will cuts Dorothea off in the event she should marry Ladislaw, marry him, after little more than a year of widowhood, she does.

45

In spite of the visible warm sympathy with which the novelist brings about this second marriage, she is at pains to insist that it finally closes the door through which Dorothea might have passed to service of a great cause. Dorothea becomes known as a wife and mother. She often feels that there is something better she might do if only she herself were better and she knew better. But her girlhood desire to escape from her own ignorance, to grow learned and to do good, is now for ever baffled. Like Lydgate, she has been brought to renunciation and resignation. In this way each of the two chief marriages in *Middlemarch* has a complementary significance. That of the one reinforces that of the other, and vice versa.

Needless to say, however, the whole value of the novel depends on what the significance is.

Now George Eliot's theories of life—which were not delivered to her by a great tradition but were her own—she expounded too explicitly for us to be in any uncertainty regarding the way in which she expected readers to find the story of the two marriages significant, the way in which she expected the story to prove moving. In her view, it was a sad limitation on human existence that two characters capable of such devotion to impersonal ends as are Lydgate and Dorothea should be debarred from the service of mankind by the play of their own human needs, as a result of their own human frailty—their blindness and their impetuousness—and by the poverty of education. She clearly intended in consequence that everything which conspires to drive both Lydgate and Dorothea, in choosing to marry as they do, to choose wrongly, should appear to the reader as regrettable, and that the reader should be moved by the novel to a feeling of sadness. This intention, it is evident, moreover, she was convinced she had fulfilled.

At the risk of seeming not to play the game of literary criticism according to the rules, I want to suggest that this intention of the author's was wrong. I believe that she wrought better than she knew. I consider that, necessarily taking the novel as it is, the reader may interpret it otherwise, and that to do so is to the reader's advantage. I think that, far from being left with a feeling of sadness at the account of the renunciations to which Lydgate and Dorothea

46

are brought, the reader from these can take heart. It seems to me that Lydgate with his ambition to succeed in medical research, and Dorothea with her yearning to do somehow good to the world, may be viewed as akin to people in real life who spend their days in pursuing what they do not truly want. And this I am ready to maintain in face of the fact that it was something which apparently the novelist herself could not see. It requires an outsider—i.e. some reader—to understand that Lydgate, in renouncing research for his wife's sake, and Dorothea, in losing all chance of a life of impersonal abnegation because she is in love, are the subjects of biographies in which one wrong choice commands later a second that is right. This, and not the defeat of lofty ambitions, is what, in the novel, ought to move the reader; and it is, I suggest, infinitely more moving. It ought to pierce the reader's heart with its poignancy.

Perhaps I may be allowed to mention that it was as the result of a conversation with the French critic, Charles Du Bos, that I came to read *Middlemarch* for the first time; because at one point in the first volume of his *Journal*, published posthumously in 1946, Du Bos states why he highly admires this novel. It is extremely rare, he says, for an imaginative writer to evince an awareness of the existence of others. But in the stories and plays of Tchekhov, in the great Tolstoyan novels, and, above all, in the novels of George Eliot, it is just this awareness that the reader beholds and has brought home to him. There is not only a protagonist, but an antagonist also. Du Bos puts *Middlemarch* well above its author's other novels; and if what he says in his *Journal* is true at all, of *Middlemarch* it must be especially and pre-eminently true.

However, in order to agree with him regarding its capital importance in fiction, we need to understand clearly what he means by 'the existence of others'. He can only mean, I feel, that in *Middlemarch* especially the novelist has depicted the leading characters, Lydgate and Dorothea, as each conscious of a moral relation to others, or, rather, to one other individual. That is to say, as characters in a novel seldom do, each of the two leading characters in *Middlemarch* grows conscious of the needs of another and of the claims of that other upon him or her. Du Bos points out that this consciousness cannot be observed by a reader; it can only be felt.

Let us now try to see what the diagnosis implies, even though of course I cannot tell if Du Bos would have assented to what I now go on to say.

When Lydgate arrives in the town of Middlemarch, bringing with him his high ambition and his bold self-confidence, he reckons without the temptation of circumstance and the weaknesses of his own temperament. Above all, he does not allow for the possibility that another will intrude upon his life. Clearly this is a deficiency in him. To have an ambition to engage in valuable medical research is all very well. It is all very well to be gifted with the scientific temper. But neither is enough. We do not lead our lives on a desert island. We live in a human society. We are surrounded by other people. As our lives unroll, one becomes necessary to us, and sometimes more than one. We acquire a mate and perhaps children. Hence we may plan our lives as if others did not exist, as if no other life could irrupt into our own, but we then invite failure and disappointment. Lydgate tells himself plainly that he had better not marry for at least five years. Yet no sooner has he met Rosamond Vincy, the mayor's daughter, shortly after his arrival in the town of Middlemarch, than he thinks of her as a desirable companion and as lady of his house. It can only be that while he fancies that research is what he wants, his real want is of a wife and a home.

Furthermore, those other people whom we meet and who excite feelings in us, have feelings also. Like ourselves, they have ambitions and make plans. The quality of *Middlemarch* is evident as soon as the reader is shown simultaneously Rosamond's independent existence and Lydgate's failure, half in love with her though he already is, to see that she exists. It never occurs to Lydgate that his appearance in the mayoress's drawing-room may give Rosamond food for thought. But the reader is at once told that Rosamond has heard that Lydgate is 'really well connected' and that she decides she can hope for no more advantageous match.

Lydgate is possibly no more self-centred than anybody else. Certainly he is no more self-centred than Rosamond. Yet it is only if he were less self-centred than he is that he could be aware at this stage of Rosamond's independent existence. It is only then that he might perceive that he is already inside the toils of her scheming. That does not mean that he is powerless. For although we have to suppose that the future is being determined by the desires and wills of others as well as by our own, we cannot suppose that this deprives us of all decision. Whatever plans Rosamond may form, it still rests with Lydgate to fall in or not to fall in with them. But already once before he has, we learn, been betrayed into impetuous folly as regards women. While studying in Paris he made a fool of himself over an actress. Now in Middlemarch this previous unfortunate experience is one from which he is incapable of profiting. One trouble is that in his own eyes he is still no more than an admirer of Rosamond's. That is why he thinks he is safe, or, rather, does not see whither he is being led. The Paris misadventure has not shown him how he needs to guard against his susceptibility. No doubt he cannot avoid meeting Rosamond now and then, but he deliberately goes to her father's house more often than is demanded of him. It only requires an occasion on which he finds Rosamond alone, and she weeps and displays an entirely natural weakness, and he has fallen in love. As she has been bent from the first on marrying him, an engagement follows. Once engaged, there is no drawing back. For Rosamond's methods may be passive, her purpose is unshakable. Her father's opposition she overcomes by ignoring it. It is important that the adamantine vein in her character should be visible here before the marriage, as it is going to be a decisive factor in determining Lydgate's later renunciation.

But it is he who makes the circumstances in which her will prevails—he and his character, he and his temperament. The reasons which he has hitherto admitted against an early marriage he now brushes aside without a qualm. He has only £800 capital, but he never tells Rosamond that in marrying they will have to start small. He not only takes an expensive house; he spends more than he can afford in furnishing it. Furthermore, in addition to living modestly, he should be conciliating patients. At times, however, he is tactlessly outspoken. To his own prejudices he is as strongly attached as the townspeople are to theirs, but while he wants his respected, theirs he disregards, applying his innovations with intransigence. As the reader is told, he is 'a little too self-confident and disdainful'; his mind, though 'distinguished', 'is a little spotted with commonness'. Yet another weakness is working against him. His 'better energies are liable to lapse down the wrong channel under the influence of transient solicitations'. That side by side with all this he should unswervingly feel a great tenderness for Rosamond is to be put to his credit, even though it contributes as much as anything to shape the sequel.

His embarrassments increase, and there is no prospect of adventitious relief. The day arrives when he has to give a bill of sale on his furniture. Hitherto his tenderness for Rosamond has made him avoid inflicting his worries upon her. Now, however, there is to be an inventory, and she must be told of it. She does not make the telling easy. She speaks in 'her silvery neutral way', and goes back to her place without looking at him. Her prime concern is that nobody shall be able to find fault with her. At this point both possibly feel farther away from one another than they have ever felt before.

As he communicates his bad news, the sense of sharing his trouble causes him to grow again tender. But all she says is: 'What can *I* do?' and she throws into the words as much neutrality as they will hold. They fall 'like a mortal chill on Lydgate's roused tenderness'. Then she says she will ask her father for money. He forbids it, and she weeps. When she has calmed herself, she reverts to her favourite plan, that they should leave Middlemarch and that he should go into practice near his baronet uncle. That has been all along what seems to her desirable. He rejects it impatiently. In the end 'an appearance of accord' is momentarily recovered, but it is only an appearance and it is only momentary.

The emotive power of the scene is due to two elements. One is Rosamond's otherness—she cannot see that she may not be in the right—and the second is Lydgate's need of her with her otherness and in spite of it. A little later he upbraids her for acting behind his back. She is silent. He goes on speaking, and she weeps. Passivity, silence, tears—those are her weapons; and in view of Lydgate's tenderness for her they are deadly. He now looks at her, and feels a 'half-maddening sense of helplessness'. He moderates his words, and still she says nothing. He demands an admission of error and a promise of amendment. She quickly detects in his voice the tone of a request. Quietly but firmly she refuses both. 'You have not made my life pleasant of late', she says. Thereupon he has to recognise that she feels aggrieved. That is her victory. She at once feels that he has softened. 'I only wished to prevent you from hurrying us into wretchedness without any necessity', she says. And her tears come again. Lydgate replies by drawing his chair near to hers and pressing her delicate head against his cheek. He has to go out again, and on his way he tells himself that it is ten times harder for her than for him. He is in an excusing mood. He now thinks of her as if she were an animal of another species. 'Nevertheless she had mastered him', the novelist says.

It is, then, partly because Rosamond has won that they presently leave the town of Middlemarch. They go because she has been determined all the time that they shall go, and Lydgate is powerless to oppose her. It is suggested to him— by Dorothea—'Suppose you stayed here though only with the friendship of a few, the evil feeling towards you would gradually die out'. He replies: 'I can't see my wife miserable. She has set her mind against staying. She wishes to go. The troubles she has had here have wearied her'. He goes on to admit that he is no longer sure what it would be possible for him to do, having Rosamond as his wife. In the admission, the meaning of the words 'She had mastered him' is brought home to the reader. But that is not the whole explanation why the couple go away.

Long before this point, the illusions with which Lydgate marries are dispelled. He has been brought to realise how far he is from being in reality Rosamond's ideal, and the realisation, the novelist says, is 'like a sad milestone marking how far he had travelled from his old dreamland in which Rosamond would reverence her husband's mind'. He begins 'to distinguish between that imagined adoration and the attraction towards a man's talent because it gives him prestige'. But, notwithstanding his disillusion, he goes on loving Rosamond and comes to love her in herself, different though she is from the woman he vaguely imagines to begin with. He loves the woman of flesh and blood to whose company he has grown habituated. The mere sight of her is enough to contract his susceptible heart.

It will, he is said to tell himself, be bitter irony if they go on living together without love for one another. He has faced the first great disappointment, that the real wife does not correspond to the ideal of his imagination. But the real wife, the reader learns, has 'not only her claims'; she has 'still a hold on his heart'.

'In marriage the certainty, "She will never love me much", is easier to bear than the fear, "I shall love her no more". '

Earlier it is said of him that with his endurance of 'her little claims and interruptions without impatience' and his disillusion regarding the calibre of her mind, there was mingled self-discontent. 'It always remains true that if we had been greater, circumstance would have been less strong against us.' Of this Lydgate, the novelist says, grows vaguely aware. He sees that he must now reckon with his own limitations. It is a big step forward in self-knowledge and in experience of life. There is an occasion when he expects Rosamond to say that she does not believe in his disgrace. Instead she once more proposes her favourite remedy, that they should go away. Lydgate feels, the reader is told, 'miserably jarred'. He leaves the room. Thereupon the novelist says in her own person:

'Perhaps if he had been strong enough to persist in his determination to be the more because she was the less, that evening might have had a better issue. If his energy could have borne down that check, he might still have wrought on Rosamond's vision and will.'

She then states her conviction that natures even inflexible or peculiar cannot be regarded as certain to resist the effect 'from a more massive being than their own'. Undoubtedly it would move a reader more if George Eliot had been able to show this instead of merely saying it. To show it, however, would not have been easy. At least she makes clear that Lydgate lacks 'a more massive being' than his wife's. He is worn down. His energy falls short. That is the ultimate compulsion that drives him to bid farewell to his ambitions. But he does preserve his marriage, and in this gain from his sacrifice resides the essence of his drama. Of course he regrets renouncing the scientific triumphs which he once pictured as in store for him. But it does not follow that had he retained and cultivated his interest in research he would have made valuable discoveries. That what we give up would have, did we retain it, the results we anticipate is something of which we can never be sure. What Lydgate relinquishes is therefore the uncertain. It is the certain to which he holds on—that indisputable love for his wife which he already has, and the supporting warmth of her presence at his side. He makes a wrong choice in marrying as he does. But the first choice, though wrong, commands later a second that is right. As we read *Middlemarch*, it is, I contend, in our realisation of this, and not in that of the melancholy of his renunciation, that our feelings should be quickened.

Likewise, in the biography of Dorothea, what the reader can find to be most moving is not that she becomes merely a wife and mother and is precluded by her ignorance from ever fulfilling her girlhood dreams of helping on the good of the world. What the reader can find most moving is, I suggest, that, beginning as one of the 'new women'—the women who were to hammer at the gate of the professions and clamour for the vote—she ends up as an 'old-fashioned womanly woman'. This is indeed very moving, not merely because to be a wife and mother is to be something more universal and fundamental than a social benefactress, but also because Dorothea is depicted winning the haven of her second marriage through the exercise of moral magnanimity. That 'intensity of her religious disposition', of which the novelist speaks in the beginning, gives to her humdrum destiny at the end a touching grandeur. This is why I feel that the gratification of her love, not the frustration of her dreams, ought to stir the reader, and stir the reader's heart not to sadness but to hope.

In Dorothea's development too, the felt existence of others has its influence One day Casaubon, in his jealousy, rebuffs her, and she goes to her room hotly indignant at his unjust behaviour. But as she sits solitary, and calm returns to her, a vital realisation dawns. She realises that Casaubon's outburst has been the cry of pain of a proud and lonely spirit lacerated by the cruel stab of recognition that the merit and importance to which it pretends are not only denied to it, but are also without warrant. She realises, that is to say, Casaubon's otherness; and although it is otherness different from that which Lydgate comes to recognise in Rosamond, the realisation is equally tinged with pathos. For she sees that it means Casaubon's wound is deeper than hers, and, unlike hers, beyond healing, She sees that his need of the balm of sympathy is correspondingly acute. Seeing all this, she is able to dominate herself. She goes to the head of the stairs to wait in the dark for him to come up.

This first victory which she wins over herself is but the prelude to another more momentous. Nearly a year after Casaubon's death, Lydgate, moved in his distress by an offer of help on her part, is brought to confide in her. He says: 'The fact is, this trouble has come upon her [Rosamond] confusedly. We have not been able to speak to each other about it.' The disclosure leads Dorothea to offer to go to see Rosamond.

Now Ladislaw for more than a year has been living in the town of Middlemarch and during this time he has been a friend of the Lydgates. Often Rosamond and he have sung duets together. When the news at last reaches her that Lydgate is mixed up in a scandal, she allows herself to imagine in her misery that Ladislaw cares for her—hopelessly of course, but nevertheless desperately. She sends for him. He is alone with her when Dorothea, by mistake, is shown into the parlour. Preoccupied only with her errand of help, Dorothea enters, and is confronted by the sight of Ladislaw clasping Rosamond's hands. They are obviously saying something intimate to one another. The sight is a great shock to Dorothea; for Ladislaw has avowed earlier that he loves her, and she has admitted to herself that she loves him. In the circumstances she can only go away again —too disturbed to speak.

Back at home her first sensations are of pain and regret. 'I did love him', she sobs. But she does not stop at this. As on the occasion of Casaubon's outburst, she grows conscious of otherness—this time the otherness of Rosamond. She thinks of Rosamond's sad plight, and also of Lydgate. She feels that a home is in danger of being wrecked. Finally, after struggling with herself during the whole of an all-night vigil, she brings herself to decide to call on Rosamond again. The decision has two consequences. Not only is Rosamond painfully aware that the town is at present against her husband, but also the day before, Ladislaw, on being left with Rosamond after Dorothea's retreat, has vented on her his disgust and scorn. His anger reduces her to a state in which she is glad to have the shelter and comfort of her husband still awaiting her. Thus when Dorothea pays her second visit, the sight of her is to Rosamond like a strong cordial. Rosamond feels that if she tells Dorothea the truth concerning Ladislaw, she will put herself right. He had held her hands to tell her that he could not love her, because he loved another. So the result of a call which was decided upon only after a long and painful struggle is twofold. Rosamond's pain is assuaged, and Dorothea undergoes a revulsion of feeling that is more than joy. A little while afterwards Ladislaw cannot refrain from calling on Dorothea, and he discovers that she has been reassured on his account. Now she cannot bear to let him go. She too has made her second choice that is right.

Stephen Spender

WHAT IS MODERN IN
MODERN POETRY

Some people talk as though they were in favour of all contemporary works of art being 'modern'. In this case they praise every contemporary achievement which they regard as modern and they dislike any work done by any contemporary artist which does not in some way aim at being modern. At the other extreme, there are those who regard everything which aims at being modern in art with disfavour. They like what is traditional and old and they dislike modern art.

Now there is a certain mysteriousness in all this talk about what is modern in art. My purpose here is to consider what being modern means in one particular art, poetry, though the modernism which I analyse in poetry has its parallels also in painting and in music.

Those people who support the modern think of modernism in poetry as distinctly an aim. By modern, they do not just mean being contemporary. They mean, rather, writing in a special way, writing about a special subject-matter; rejecting certain old forms of writing poetry and using perhaps *vers libre*; or even discovering what are called 'new forms' or using old forms in an entirely new way. Being modern is an idea at once strong and generalised. It is so strong that one might almost say that in most minds there is by now an idea of what is modern which contains its classical examples. For instance, Walt Whitman is 'modern' because he wrote in free verse. Rimbaud on the other hand often uses conventional forms without, as it were, the slightest regard for their conventions. Gerard Manley Hopkins wrote sonnets which, although strictly and technically sonnets, yet observed none of the principles of development which most of his contemporaries expected from the sonnet. There are already many classical examples of modern art, not only in poetry, but still more in painting and music (the impressionists, the Post-impressionists, the music of Stravinsky written before the last war, etc.). One has only to mention these works to see that they retain their essentially *modern* character. Modernism does not mean just being fashionable, up-to-date. It is quite conceivable even that modernism as an aim might become démodé and out of date (as it has done in Soviet Russia), though it would remain nevertheless a part of the now historic modern movement. In fact, I should say that the generation of writers living today is less modernist than that living in 1909. We who live in 1948 are not as futurist as the Futurists in 1909 thought we would be.

I think that two methods are necessary in order to analyse and criticise the concept *modern* in poetry. The first method is a process of psycho-analysis. The idea of that which is modern exists in our own minds, it is a powerful motive of many artists. It has the force of a complex, even sometimes of a neurosis. It may be a blind compulsive force which has not been brought out into the conscious light of criticism. Therefore I shall try to psycho-analyse my own idea of what is modern, as an aim which I recognise in the work of others and in my own work. The second method of understanding the modern aim is to state some theory of the relation of the contemporary artist to the world in which we live, which will discuss modernism as a poetic method of interpreting contemporary phenomenon in terms of the imagination.

I begin first then with the psycho-analytic approach, and I take myself, as a typical case-history. I can discover in my own case a preoccupation with the idea of being modern which illuminates for me the very personal and often incompletely explained obsession with the idea of being a 'modern' poet which one finds in remarks of Apollinaire, some asides of the surrealists, the symbolists, the imagists, etc.

I can remember very distinctly walking along a road in Hampstead, London, when I was twelve years old and suddenly becoming preoccupied with the idea of writing a novel which would move in scarcely perceptible gradations

57

from prose to rhythmic prose, from rhythmic prose to free verse, from free verse to rhyme and fixed forms. My idea was that the book should have an enormous range of form and yet no fixed form. Of course, this idea was very crude, and unless one can elaborate it much further it is without intrinsic interest. And here I am concerned simply with one personal, subjective aspect of it, that at this early stage I was seized with an overwhelming desire to create something entirely new in a form which was entirely new. And it is significant to me that the idea of novelty occurred to me firstly as a revolution in form, because I am now going to suggest that there are three stages in the development of the modern poetic movement: the first is the revolution in the form of poetry; the second is the introduction of a modern subject-matter into poetry; and the third is the development of a modern attitude towards the experiences contained in modern poetry.

To return now to my own crude experiences of the modern impulse: when I was eighteen and wrote a great deal of very bad verse, I had a passion for introducing slums, gasworks, factories, pylons and all such modern symbols into my poems, though I was not able to integrate this material into a larger poetic experience. Later, when I was living in Berlin in the later nineteen-twenties until 1933, I made the discovery that there is a certain attitude towards experience which enables the artist to weave the most modern material into his work, so that it becomes human and not merely mechanical. I found this attitude not so much in poetry at that time, as in some music—particularly the music of Hindemith and Alban Berg . . . and in the cinema, particularly in the early Russian films, such as *Potemkin, Seven Days which Shook the World, Earth,* and—perhaps the Russian film in which it made its final appearance—*The Way Into Life.* I shall try later on to enlarge on this modern attitude: but for the moment let me describe it as a kind of tragic gaiety, rising in the early Russian films to a tragically heroic optimism. In the later Russian films this sense of the tragic is replaced by a mechanical, official heroism and optimism, which is no longer what I call modern. In fact, although my using the word 'modern' may appear rather arbitrary, most people would understand what I mean when I say that the Russian film has stopped being 'modern' since 1935. Before that date, from 1925 to 1935 the Russian film was definitely part of a modernist movement which extended to all the arts.

Now, leaving my own personal experience aside, I find that there is a parallel development of modernism in poetry. First we have the *vers libre* breakdown of the regular forms in which poetry was written. There follow attempts to create new forms in poetry, new patterns, new arrangements of rhyme. A revolution in poetry follows the pattern of a revolution in society. The old forms break down because it is felt that, besides being worn out, they are incapable of being adapted to the new material of contemporary life. Then there is an attempt to set up a régime of new forms which are better suited to modern conditions. Aragon's essay in defence of rhyme is a characteristic attempt to set up a new poetic régime after a poetic revolution.

In the English language, Walt Whitman is the classic example of the modern poetic revolutionary. He was conscious of the youth, the vastness, the potentialities of the young America of the nineteenth century. He was engulfed in the epic struggle of the war of the North against the South. He found the perfect hero, the Aeneas of his Aeneid, in President Lincoln. In this situation and with such material, he found that the poems of contemporary American poets were faded drawing-room imitations of the weaker followers of the English romantic movement. He decided, therefore, that America must have its own poetry which must break away completely from Europe. Walt Whitman's free verse is the American War of Independence projected formally into literature.

Nevertheless, the subject matter and the sensibility of Whitman are not essentially modern. In sensibility, he was perhaps closer to Tennyson than to any other of his contemporaries, and Tennyson recognised this in his admiration of Whitman. His subject matter is Whitman himself, war, the American epic. Occasionally Whitman is audacious, for example, in his attitude towards sex, but there is nothing modern about such audacity; many poets have shown courage in their erotic and even obscene writings. Occasionally, he writes poems which are immense lists of the occupations of Americans, the geography of America, and

59

so on. In a way these poems of Whitman are impressive, in another way they are boring, but the point is that they are not modern, because they do not become effectively integrated into Whitman's poetic sensibility. They remain as external as the names in a Directory. Whitman was a revolutionary in form, but his sensibility and his material are essentially traditional.

Baudelaire, whose use of form is surprisingly traditional, conventional even, is far more modern in the effect of his material on his sensibility, than Whitman. He was above all the poet who contributed to European poetry the experience of the boredom, the humanity, the ugliness and the beauty of the modern city.

In one his essays Eliot wrote that the noise of the petrol engine had modified the rhythmic sensibility of contemporary human beings. Thus when one speaks of the 'modern' in poetry, one does not mean that a poet may refer to a steam engine, a motor-car, a gasworks, a slum, a telephone bell, but that these things have in some way become a part of his poetic sensibility so that he speaks to his contemporaries in a language which is, in the subtlest shade of sounds and use of imagery, a contemporary language of people whose ears and eyes are surrounded by such mechanical appliances. To be modern does not mean either to write in free verse or in alexandrines. The alexandrines of Baudelaire have in their most hidden rhythm an echo of the city which one would not expect to find in the free verse of Walt Whitman. The astonishingly revolutionary technique of Whitman expresses an idealised vision and a delicate love of nature which we find in certain English poets such as Clare, and, at his best, Tennyson.

In a general sense there has always been a modern movement in English poetry. It would be interesting, for example, to study the development of the blank verse line through Marlowe, Shakespeare and the later Elizabethans such as Ford, Webster and Tourneur, to see how within the sound of those ten syllables the stiffness of Marlowe's *Faustus* melted to the moonlit calm of Shakespeare's fantastic comedies, how in the later Shakespeare and the later Elizabethans the same line echoed the collapse of the Elizabethan self-confidence and the distresses of the time which followed.

Such a sensibility does not reveal itself merely in scenes portrayed but in the sound of the syllables.

To be modern, in the sense of which I speak, is therefore not just a contemporary phenomenon. What is contemporary is the insistence on modernism as an artistic aim. The Greeks always wanted to be new, people at all times have wanted to be fashionable, certain epochs have wished to be revolutionary. But being *modern*, as I am trying to describe it, is something different from this. It is an endeavour consciously to place the interior world of the creative imagination in a certain relationship with the contemporary environment. And this aim can only result from the feeling that there is an existing relationship which is unsatisfactory. I want now to discuss this relationship of the imaginative world created by contemporary poetry to the real world of modern life by which we are surrounded. In order to understand the aims of modern poetry one has to have something like a theory of the relationship of poetry to the world.

Let us first say that there is a difference between one poet's theory about his own poetry and a theory about the whole of poetry. For the individual poet the problem of his poetry is comparatively simple. It is to write the poetry which he is able to write, to develop his gifts and to be aware of his limitations. He has to accept the fact that he may not be able to write the kind of poetry which he thinks ought to be written. Therefore when I speak of modernism in poetry I am not criticising individual poets because they are not modern. I am merely stating that there appears to be a general function possible to the whole of modern poetry which is to integrate into the world of poetry the ugliness, the fantastic beauty, the apparent inhumanity of those phenomena which are sometimes called 'the machine age'.

Some poets have tried to strengthen their own poetry and perhaps also the whole of poetry by introducing this iron, steam and fire into the tissues of poetic language. But in doing this, they are not, of course, just trying to make their poetry more forceful and mechanical by adding to poetry the superhuman strength of machinery. The modern movement is not a movement to make poetry inhuman. It is rather a movement which refuses to accept the discouraging idea that the modern world of the machine age is in some

61

way inhuman. It takes the view that everything created by human beings is material available to poetry, because every machine, every war, every slum, every organisation, every new invention is a crystallisation within the external world of inward human wishes, fears, passions. To say that a machine is a crystallisation of such essentially human forces is to say that the concrete shape of this crystallisation—the machine itself—is a poetic symbol for all those human passions.

A description of a great modern town in imaginative terms which have a psychological truth as great as that contained in a Greek tragedy is entirely possible. One could regard the whole of a great city, such as Paris, as an enormous complex of dreams intermingled and lying over each other like washes of water-colour on a sheet of paper. The dreams of the past project themselves into the present. The dreams of Napoleonic glory, for example, have left their symbols, such as the Arc de Triomphe, which subsist through the dark shadow of German power during the Occupation, and the little flame of the Unknown Warrior burns under the jackboots of the German dream. In some quarters of the city, the lives of the poor, that is to say the dreams and aspirations of the poor, are entangled in the more rigid and powerful lines of the dreams of their exploiters. But nevertheless it is all a dream, and the only hope of humanity is to make it dream a better dream, seek a better and less selfish kind of happiness, and banish nightmares.

The whole of human history is such a dream, and theories of human history, such as the Marxist theory of historic materialism, are simply theories of dream interpretation applied on the enormous scale to the whole of society, instead of on the minute scale of the human individual. The Marxist, indeed, agrees with the Freudian that the motive of the human dream is the fulfilment of a wish of an egoistic and material kind.

The problem of our lives, whether we consider ourselves as individuals or as whole societies is that we live on two levels. One level is the inner, changeable, extremely fluid level of fantasy and personality, the other is the outward level in which we interpret our fantasies into those actions which I call crystallisations. There is a gulf between the individual world of fantasy and the outer world of crystallised fantasies because the inner world is a constantly changing scene of the imaginative life, and the outer world is a very fixed scene. The dream of the machines and cities and power politics and wars which we project into the outer world is one from which we cannot wake up. And when we crystallise a nightmare for ourselves and when at the same time we realise that we are hopelessly frozen in this nightmare from which we cannot wake up, we start saying that it is inhuman, mechanical, outside ourselves, and impossible to be translated into terms of the fluid human imagination.

Now I would not agree with certain critics that it is the function of the poet to change the human dream, for the simple reason that when one starts trying to change the dream, one ceases to be a dreamer and becomes occupied with the external process of machines and organisations into which the dream has crystallised. One becomes a social realist or a propagandist. Change takes place on the level of action. There comes a moment when the change in the imaginative life has to pass on to this other level and take place in the world of architecture and machines and organisations, and when it does that it ceases to have the quality of fluid imagination and becomes crystallised into constructive and external tasks.

No. The function of poetry is to re-create for us the symbolic aspect of things: to show us that human inventions symbolize human passions: to uncrystallise institutions and inventions and actions so that we see them again as human desires, human fears, expressions of human needs.

When we say that the contemporary world is inhuman, impersonal, mechanical, all we mean is that the crystallisation of modern needs into machinery, organisations, and so on, is far more complex and vast today than it was in the past. It is so complex that when we look at the world around us we find it filled with organisations and inventions which seem to have lost their original personal and human impulse. We are surrounded everywhere by organisations which instead of being the means by which we can organise our wishes, the symbols upon which we can concentrate our imagination, become means of organising our lives and robbing us of our humanity.

This being the position, there are two general tendencies in modern art. One is to shrink from this world which appears to be so inhuman and so impersonal into a smaller world of the personal, the private, the obscure, the remote, the individual, the whimsical and the inconsequential. The other is to endeavour to relate the life of the imagination to the world of vast inhuman-seeming organisations and inventions which modern humanity has created.

Often these two impulses of shrinking and expansion exist side by side in the same poet. In some poets, there are periods of expansion followed by periods of shrinking. For example, W. H. Auden in his earlier work brought a highly individual interpretation of Freudianism combined with Marxism to bear on the modern world. In these poems one has a picture of an England which is a kind of hospital of crowds who owe their humanity to the fact that they are interpreted as being ill by the poet who is a kind of mental doctor. Their physical environment of slums and factories and their social environment of unemployment, war and revolution are a series of neurotic projections which unite the whole of humanity in a kind of purgatory. Beyond this purgatory there gleams the faint light of a revolutionary dawn which will create a better world for humanity in which everyone will fulfil his or her individuality by having a satisfactory place in the social structure. There, the instruments of production, instead of being the vague wilderness which engulfs humanity in the chaos of mis-shapen dreams, will be peaceful irrigating rivers flowing through society, bearing their gifts of milk and honey.

This is a vision from which Auden has retreated into a certain mysticism in his later work. His reasons for retreating are fairly obvious. The social vision of the poet is certainly a way of forming an imaginative and humanizing vision of our modern life, but unfortunately it is compromised by the disagreeable fact that society does not seem to be moving towards a socialist paradise. If we are to form a poetically true picture of human life as a unity of consciousness underlying the diverse and broken up structure of external crystallisations of our time, a socialist vision is not enough. For such a vision consists of pretending that the external disunity is going to cease at some point and we are going to return to a kind of life in which there is a harmony of the inner dream with the outward appearance. But we have to take it into account that this may not happen. Utopianism or even social realism does not uncrystallise the world of crystallised impulses in which we live. It merely explains them, and the truth of the explanation is dependent on external events, not on the power of the imagination. To imagine things truly we must imagine them as they are.

There is one great poem which is the supreme example of a modern poem in English. That is T. S. Eliot's *The Waste Land*. *The Waste Land* which was written shortly after the war of 1914–1918 is simply a vision of chaos: it is a statement in bare and fragmentary terms of a vision of the present condition of humanity. Eliot is confronted here with the problem I have stated, which is to create the modern, apparently inhuman and therefore unimaginable environment in such terms that we see it as an expression of our human life and feelings, impulses and traditions. He does so by the extremely successful device of confronting some vivid invocation of the past with an equally vivid invocation of some present scene which corresponds significantly to the past scene. We move from an invocation of classical mythology to a conversation in a London pub: from a passage which reminds us of the passage in Shakespeare's *Antony and Cleopatra* where there is the famous description of Cleopatra seated in her barge on the Nile, to a sordid love scene in a boarding-house. There is a wonderful description of that stretch of the river Thames which Spenser celebrated in his great poem *Prothalamium*, which Eliot contrasts with the modern Thames, sweating with oil and tar, with its banks covered with sandwich papers, crowded with holiday-makers. But when I say Eliot contrasts the past with the present I weaken the impression of his effect, which is not so much that of contrast but of juxtaposition. Everything in *The Waste Land* is juxtaposed: a great past drawn from all ages, from Greece, from India and from the England of Elizabeth with a sordid modern chaos of his time; a great literature, with an ignoble use of language; a great mythology drawn from paganism, from Buddhism and from Christianity, with an era of unbelief; ravishing and pure beauty is juxtaposed with squalid ugliness.

E   65

The effect of *The Waste Land* is overwhelming. It is a poem which certainly tells us that it is possible to invent a form in poetry which integrates the experience of the modern world within the human imagination: it is possible also to invent a style, concentrated, fragmentary and rapid, which is surely the style of our age. One finds this same power of concentration in Apollinaire and in Eluard.

But here I am brought up against the third problem of a modern poetry, which is the problem of the attitude of the poet towards the experiences of our time which are peculiarly modern. I have shown how Auden retreated from an attitude which, however critical and analytical, was nevertheless utopian in that it presupposed some great change which would introduce a new harmony between the inner and the outer life. The attitude of Eliot in *The Waste Land* is complete despair, complete nihilism. This utterly negative attitude enabled him to realise the vision of that moment, but it did not lead anywhere further. *The Waste Land* is *Le Voyage au Bout de La Nuit* and beyond the night there is either the dawn or abyss and silence, or else perhaps just an interminable continuation of *The Waste Land* which suggests a way of looking at things which is static and incapable of development. With Eliot the solution was a return to Christianity, but this return implied a certain retreat from the reality of *The Waste Land*. The significance of Eliot's further development is that while he continued to despair of society, he discovered in Christianity the possibility of personal salvation. *The Waste Land* tells us how much we are involved in this world, his later work how little we are involved in it. *The Waste Land* is the vision of a moment in time, the later poems are concerned with escaping from time into timelessness.

The result is that in the later poems, although Eliot continues to use a modern imagery, he is no longer so interested in the imaginative interpretation of the modern world. The modern imagery is simply used by way of vivid illustration to show how it is possible for the individual in search of salvation to escape from the modern world. Thus Eliot, who began by being a poet influenced by Baudelaire, Apollinaire and Laforgue in their interpretation of the life of the individual within the modern industrial environment, ceases to be part of that movement. The Church can only condemn the modern world and show us that we are not creatures of its environment.

Perhaps the most successful and characteristic attitude of the poet who seeks consciously to be modern, is to be found in the work of Apollinaire. This is the attitude which I have called one of 'tragic gaiety'. The poet dramatises himself as the modern man who sees in all human inventions potentialities of experiencing new sensations, creating new worlds, new forms. He sees an aeroplane in the sky and he identifies it with his own spirit, he looks down on Paris at dawn with the eyes of the pilot of the aeroplane. He measures himself against the machinery of war and he is glad when he triumphs over war's misery. When he is finally killed one feels that he has succumbed to an excess of the machine age as gladly as he would succumb to an excess of alcohol. The speed and wit and gleam of his poetry borrow something from machinery and at the same time remain human. The result of this constant measuring of himself against the modern world in all its most violent aspects is that the poet never takes either himself or his poetry too seriously. Every poem is a flight. Although one feels that the poet is a pilot in control of his poem, he is also carried on the engine of an impulse which is never quite his own impulse. A poem is something that happens to him rather than something that grows out of him and he never travels quite to the centre of his experience, so that every poem has a certain carelessness, a quality of neither being completely finished or even completely begun. Nevertheless every poem shines like steel.

But this gaiety of Apollinaire is also tragic, because one feels that the poet is after all carried from one experience to another by these forces outside himself. At one moment he is in one country and at another in another, and although his gaiety accepts and is glad to be carried away, nevertheless it is a sad journey with very few resting-places.

This tragic gaiety is characteristic of what I would call a transitional attitude towards the modern world. It is to be found in those early Russian films, which I have already mentioned, and as far as I can judge from translations it has its counterpart in poems of Maiakovsky and in *The Twelve* of Alexander Blok.

This episode illustrates well enough a certain attitude towards machinery. The machine is regarded partly as an extension of the human body, partly as a joke which can be treated with a good-humoured contempt. That was the mood of the Russians towards the tractor at a certain moment. But the machinery which looks like a romantic fate ends by being a tragic fate sending everyone to the war in its tanks and its aeroplanes.

Here I have simply discussed certain aspects of the aims of modernism in poetry. To me the poets and artists who endeavoured to be modern—in the senses which I have been discussing—are heroes, because they have tried to make us understand in terms of our imagination the environment which we have blindly made for ourselves. They have tried to open our eyes to what we are doing.

What they have not succeeded in is to create an attitude towards that environment other than the tragi-comic one of acceptance. Yet it is something that they have tried to make us see our world of great organisations, great machines, great industries, great wars, as a projection into reality of our own consciousness and not as inhuman forces controlling our lives. Nevertheless, although our environment is projected from ourselves, there is a sense in which we are dominated by it. Therefore it is not enough just to make us see the situation of the world we have made for ourselves, we must also have an attitude towards that situation if it is to be completely significant. This is where the poets who wished to be modern have failed. The consequence of that failure is a retreat from modernism into the religion of Eliot, the abtruse metaphysical thought of the later work of Auden, the surrealism, the personalism, the new romanticism of many other writers.

But there is a possibility that in the next years there will develop a completely new attitude towards our industrial civilisation. Recent discoveries make it perfectly clear to us that our whole civilisation can either be destroyed in another war or that it must be organised in the interests of the whole of humanity. Until recently we have had to take up an attitude towards what seemed to be a mechanical fate imposed on us by the development of our inventions. It was possible to say that our inner human condition was responsible for that fate, but saying so did not help us to control it. Today a new responsibility has been forced upon our inner life. We are a civilisation confronted with two futures. Complete destruction or world organisation. The realisation of this choice is already affecting the whole consciousness of humanity. A phase in the whole of human history, including the arts, is being closed. And for that reason it seems worth re-examining what was the conception of the modern in our recent poetry.

ENGLISH POETRY

chosen by

Wrey Gardiner

★

Alan Ross

THE DEATH OF SHELLEY

I

By Via Reggio the waters gave the body up.

The July sea, exhausted by the storm,
released the poet on the sable beach; an arm
of green and white encircling waves
cut off the shadow from the tideless caves.

The blue sky drained the sun's still burning cup.

With Sophocles and Keats in its pockets
the drowned figure dressed for sailing
—blue jacket, nankeen trousers, white silk socks—
floated dreamily towards the beckoning rocks.

He had died so often bit by bit in life, Death
found little left to take, but the failing breath.

And the sea so close to his imagery and art
now merely isolated and wrapped round his heart.

In the end the familiar waters greeted him as a friend.

II

The long struggle of the early days, when words
were weapons not a gift, and terms in essays
caused a final rift from men, whose laws
were quite remote from changes and from needs,
ensured the later exile and the lost estate,
that caused the failure in the practice of ideas
denied him in the return home he planned too late.

But holding always to a passionate conviction
he strove through abstract truth to wrest
the social balance from the laws of God,
and put his faith in attributes that Man possessed:
though, most of all, the things he grew to hate
were blind regressive forces that convened
the laws and codes which made a cult of states,

and like a rigid and unmoving cast imprisoned
men behind a mask of statutes, whose cold hearts
enveloped life in justice without vision, the pity
and compassion lacking in the false causality
that in a compress formulates the social need;
and puts a motive into every victim's mouth
condemning him a criminal, eaten up with greed.

The inward voice must always first be heard:
so Shelley writing from the South took on himself
the lost causes and the debts his view of wealth
and property demanded—for which, despite
the double shadows of his personal life,
the drowning accusation of a wife, escaping health,
he went on paying the debt on Godwin's life.

Yet could not find the truly right equation—
love even which he found like silver, turned
within his secret mind to different deep endeavours
and did not satisfy the permanent one desire:
although in friends he found a lighter obligation,
to which without a woman's love he could aspire.

Most deeply now, through time, the poetry remains:
the interests in science and reform are part
of the larger, more complex pattern of the art
in which he crossed the boundaries of knowledge
into facts some hidden shutter of his mind released;
the ideology of verse which, in itself, made ideas aware
before the imagery grew still, or the music ceased.

And on the warm Italian shores, the meetings
on the lakes with Byron, and the constant
exchanges of delight at beauty in the eyes
of women, the lyric of his mood grew more controlled,
detailed with the experience of the landscape and the sea
whose restless beauty drew him like a state of love,
the waves' frustration on the rocks an image of humanity.

The music made him understand the suffering
and the nature of the grief that, like a ruin,
grew inside his knowledge of the world; the sound
became a fevered mirror for his mind and poetry:
the mountains and the hills, the yellow sands, in turn
drew from behind ideas the sun-drenched words
which made each intellectual concept seem to burn.

But then the century that had not grown old
but grown up almost with him and the friends
—Trelawney, Byron, Hunt—that gave
the embryonic age a myth and legend, found him,
who had not become a part of time but stood instead
outside the limits of the years, and wrote
the final line in water on his forehead.

The heat and swimming sky burned round the grave

and on the afternoon the pyre was made
they poured the wine and oil upon the flame
which lime had turned inside the skull to indigo
as light burnt out the letters of his name.

The slow process of the final death displayed
a phial of colour dancing in the air
pure and spiritual, which made the group arrayed
uncomfortable, but riveted and forced to stare.

Only Byron turned away in grief, and swimming
out to sea gazed back upon the shore
watching the flat beach and marble hills,
understanding what he had not known before.

Slowly the body was burnt into an ashen stain
the shadows in the watching eyes the only pain.

And the unburnt heart, like a poem, passed
into the mask of Antigone's still heart.

Tessa M. Sillars

THRENODY FOR A BROKEN DOLL

Count up your dead, but do not bury them.
Silence and an empty dark
Contribute and are not explicit.
The touch of hands or too much thought
Intrude the quiet of their dignity;
And self-reproach rings clamorous discordancy.

Only after a clean spell of time
Can you dig the earth around those roots
Whose growth in darkness held grave-earth
That fought its silent, smothering fight
Against a delicate developing.
(Precarious life against an odds-on death.)

Do not profane the darkness
With the molestations of a questioning mind
That pricks an interfering probe
And makes abortive new-begotten love.
And kills the third identity.

The horizontal stricture of the grave
Extinguishes discernment;
And our equivocal singleness is mocked,
Anonymous beneath trite epitaph.

Tessa M. Sillars

DARK

Shall I never
Know the sweet annihilation of my death?
And always go
Encumbered by the light and never reach
The assuaging womb comfort of the dark?

Compelled along sharp canyons where the bright
Splinters refract from polished sides
I know my need for shadow and for thorns.
The flesh knows no appeasement
Where the sword's sharp death sleeps impotent.

Where are those others—
Those obscure and muted ghosts
Of my dark kingdom
Who labour towards redeeming doom
By oblique and transitory ways?

Blind circlings that cannot intersect and make
    comparison
Hide each behind himself.
Dumb cravings find
A scant relief in trickling dissemination.
Death goes denied in partial living.

All poisons powerless to bring
The consummation of extremity
Are proved, discarded, sought again.
Alone I shall not find
My ultimate and life-destroying thing.

Wrey Gardiner

MORNING WALK

The frame of living lies across the sands
Under the sun, between cliff and tide
Where time is only the time between
The tides, the shadow under the cliff.

Empty seas are the source still of the years
Empty your mind of time and memory of death
Hunger and death and the broken dreams of humanity
Lusting for life and the forgotten voice of love.

The rock sucks and the gull feels the air
With wing curving across the pale sky.
We who are simple, sad, embittered and alone
March across the hard sands towards the silence.

We walk warily between cliff and tide wondering
Why the world is not with us, why the times
Crumble under our fingers, why the dream
Is of death and profit and loss accounts,

While the gulls circle hungrily towards the dark sea,
And leave their crazy footprints on the empty sand.

Kathleen Raine

EARTHLY LOVES

We are content to be what the spring winds awake
The life that in blue eyes and golden flowers stirs,
Content to be that moving in the grass
The May tunes into music, scent, form, colour and
    dance.

Content to sleep the sleep of death and the unborn,
To dream the unmeasured hour of lover's time
If but within the fold of night our lives are one.

Content if, flesh of our flesh, the beauty of earth,
God's ever new and ever-changing dress
In skill and mystery of love, be woven of us, and by us.

FACES

From far infinity the Christian face
Like a lens casts its image on the screen
Of time and place.
There is a bird's-flight distance in the Virgin's eyes
Where angels glide on rays.

But the face of this Greek sphinx is its own meaning
Its own interrogation, its own stone.

May Sarton

THE LION AND THE ROSE

Vision is locked in stone.
The lion in the air is gone
With the great lion of the sun.
The sky is wild and cold.
The tawny fire is gone.
The hill where love did open like a rose
Is black. It snows.

Emptiness flows.
The flowers in the heart all close
Drowned in a heavy white. Love knows
That poverty untold,
The cave where nothing grows:
The flaming lions of the flesh are gone,
Their power withdrawn.

God of the empty room,
Thy will be done. Thy will be done.
Let shine the inward sun,
The beating heart that glows
Within the skeleton,
The magic rose, the purer living gold
Shine now, grown old.

All that is young and bold,
The lion's roar, the flaming skin and wild,
Unearthly peace now cherish and enfold
And fresh sleep overcome,
That in this death-in-life, delicate, cold,
The spiritual rose
Flower among the snows

The love surpassing love.

Ruthven Todd

AUTUMN CAMPION

Curiously, considering the nearness of the frost,
I found a campion, her flower, in bloom
Among the fallen leaves, one flower, half-lost
In summer's shambles in the autumn-silent wood.

This small pink bud above the crumpled brown
Shone clearly and a claxon-throated jay
Flashed blue and rose before me: stooping down
I touched her flower but left it growing;

And all the wood seemed suddenly as bright
As if spring had come back and I was glad
Her star winked happily in autumn's night
Where, moonlike, I was faithful, and was mad.

Nicholas Moore

IN A BLACK GLASS

Who holds within her hands this trembling glass,
Ancient, Doric, that 'beautiful and sensitive face',
Who has given me something upturned to the light,
And the dark and lightless black hole;

Who has let me stir the wine with a finger
Or lift up those globes of moonlight to the heights;
Who has made a forest of pines out of the night,
And has known the dark, upthrusting child;

Who has drunk the wine from the lips of the decanter
Or in the black goblet let it rest,
And the lights sparkle from the glass, throw shadows
Upon the blank and sightless wall.

Yet there is an eye in the wall, the eye of an avenger,
Who looks upon those white, curved flanks
And the uplifted rounds, as the ancient hound
Looks slavering upon the hare's moving tail,

And the quick darting of its own tongue,
As the huntsman collects up his images into the horn
Of day and night, and the chaste, epicene Diana
Pursues doubtfully the fleeting harrier's soul.

O Fury! O round white moons! O folds between!
I am familiar with that mirrored face,
So like my own, so blank reflected there,
Featureless, dark, lost in a darkling well.

Nicholas Moore

LOVERS UNDER THE ELMS

'Nothing! thou elder brother ev'n to Shade'—Rochester

'la réalité humaine est un dépassement perpetuel
vers un coincidence avec soi qui n'est jamais donné'—Sartre

Nothing comes like a faint prick under the eyelids
Or a trick played on one by one's enemy;
Nothing becomes a giant, but is nowhere
In the air or sea or sky;

Is disease, despair, incalculable misfortune,
The line drawn thin between two loves,
The rare plant, the discoverer's expedition,
The sunlight on twin graves;

And yet is nothing; comes like a sudden cancer
Or a long spell of cold and snow,
Is always between one's hope, the lack in one's being;
Exists and does not go;

Exalts and does not help, exhausts and does not give,
Leaves by no window nor by death,
Is nothing and Nothing and nothing and always there
Between breath and breath;

Is, is nothing, alters but does not change,
A doom, one's enemy's dagger that strokes to kill,
Ranges everywhere, but is nothing, Nothing only,
Itself, immovable.

And is there in the still kiss of the beloved,
And warm like a hand between breast and breast,
Next to your eyes, your mind, between your
                                    loves, Nothing
Whom you have never faced.

Howard Sergeant

MAN MEETING HIMSELF

They are moving inwards; the circle is closing.
Tonight I have heard them again among
the houses, a million voices rising as one
in the darkness, hounding our lives with their
pitiless tongues, the voices of leaves and children
crying, as children cry, for light—where is
no light; for love, where there is only silence:

and under my feet stars like dead leaves falling
under my feet the bloodless faces staring . . .

There is one hand, five-barbed with innocence,
can start a conflagration in the breast.
There is one force can find a man his likeness
in a stone, and we have buried it with lies;
but not for ever—we have not earth enough
nor words to turn the wind back from our hearts.
Come day the rocks will open and ourselves
walk out in freedom to startle the world as men.

Look into their eyes and faces if you dare
and, if you dare, describe a victory.
Not history, not hate, flows over them.

    And this is guilt—
    man meeting himself in the night,
    and hating himself and the wind
    and the lips of the wind; the swivelling
    eye and the lies most known
    by the light, the beast in the man
    and the man in the beast and himself;
    but hating most deeply and deadly
    his hatred of self—
    to answer
    I do not know their language!

Robert Payne

THE PHOENIX

Out of that desolation we were born:
Some nest or other. Fibres of roughage,
A spark set here or there among the corn,
No sorrowing Ruth here. Here we brooded
And saw the fledglings rise on copper wings
Somewhere in Egypt where the sun burns blindly.
It might have been better in Arabia or the islands.
Better than these deserts,
Where there are no rocks nor stories,
Only the tales of the wandering shell-shocked madman
And the waters pouring.

Sion! That was another place, another burning:
Here was a nest in undiscovered country,
Fresh, new and glistening.
With preened wings once we whispered
Of how the Phoenix rose and died in flames—
Ashes and dust, so many centuries.
Now we remember the place where the sand falls,
Where the mirage comes, where the hourglass
Is: there is an awakening.
Sand moving on sand, each grain swallowing another.
A desert of sand,
But somewhere the red bird calls.

O not vainly: that would be another story.
The crystal water once flowed from the white-hot rock.
Once there were men with tents, the patriarchs sang
Round the hot fires of evening, there were the pilgrimages
And the country was not barren.
They said there was milk there, wax and honey-bees,
The rivers were white in the morning.

I have not been there: I shall go my way ungainly,
Knowing there were these things once:
A pillar of cloud in the morning, and the Phoenix singing
High on the shores of Hebron.

Take heed, for the journey is long: there is an awakening,
When the eyelids are moist as a spring, when the crystal rock
   blazing
Calls out, calls out for your weeping.
I would not have you stand there in your journey.
I would have you eternally wandering
In that hot air, gazing before you
At blue tents and the people marching.
This was the time: the bronze way of the eagles,
The sand glittering and the Phoenix nesting.

LOVE AND ETERNITY

The dreams we build in this eternity will last
For our eternal now; infinity in a small room,
And history in a present lacking both a past
And a future: our devils still those of whom
We have learned terror, those who inflicted hurt
Wilfully, and those who never learned to feel:
These are our hunting dogs to flick their dirt
In our faces, those whose laws have no repeal.

This present, darling, is both now and forever,
It is an eternity in which time is short or long
As we cut it, for each of us has shears to sever
His own share, and should his right come wrong
To ask pardon only of himself, whose only good
Lay in loving where and when he could.

14.xi.1946.

Henry Treece

Eilonwy's Song from

IVAN MORGAN
AND THE MERMAID

It seems I heard a creature howl
A thousand years ago
And came below the sea to search for it,
Some white-eyed Gelert with a thorn in's paw.

What is the sound that echoes in my head,
The thoughts that eddy through my mind
Like delicately coloured schools of fish?
The slightest whisper of reality
And they have vanished with a flash of fins.

It is peaceful here; the gay weeds droop
Like preciously fantastic fruit;
Sea-melons, pears and cucumbers
Enchant the vision. Swift eyes catch
The flutter of a wing. Look, there!
A sea-thrush leaves her five brown eggs
To fly among sea-meadows for a spell!

Yesterday I stumbled on a dell
In this dark forest, where
A galley's company had met again.
Gold ear-rings flashed and white teeth gleamed
And a boy sang plaintive songs of Spain.
Seated among great heaps of gold,
The seamen showed their wounds
And marked their charts. Not one

But thought his coral-eyes would see again,
That his next voyage had at last begun . . .
Here all is peaceful: green palms soothe
The over-burdened mind,
And rainbow-tinted mirages,
Purple, emerald and gold,
Tempt tired feet
To pass, this way and that,
Among the nodding ferns.

So deep-sea day gives place to deep-sea year,
Until at last the sleeping wanderer
Forgets all else but pearly worlds,
And sinks into an opium dream of jade.

Knights' Chorus from
IVAN MORGAN
AND THE MERMAID

Under the sea,
Among the coral courts,
We loiter who are shut out from the world;
Watching the febrile crabs at their sad trade
Scuttering across the sea's deserted bed
Or leaving their quaint runes among the rocks;
We see the tropic weed put out its hand
To roll the Spanish sailor's skull
Hither and thither, like a ghastly ball;
And the green galleons, shifting with the tide,
Playground for darting mackerel
And cavern for the squid,
Scattering a golden harvest to the sand . . .

We loll among the rotting shields,

Leaning from wrecked pavilions to stare
Up to the passing keels,
The fishing boats,
Wondering if our company will grow
Before the neap-tide comes again.

We see the tiny packets march,
Each on its lawful errand, and we sigh
That men may move unhindered in the light,
While we stroll, stagnant, through a wilderness
Of bottle-green and pearl-eyed desolation,
Inventing history to salve ambition's wound,
Creating glory from a fancied dream
To staunch heart-blood's quick flow,
Thinking of the red cattle and the white cattle
And the coloured flags
Fluttering in the wind.

Oh, we are left, doomed dreamers in the dusk,
Forgotten by the very sons we saved,
Less than a starfish
Or a gaudy shell;
Too dark for Heaven
And too light for Hell!

Alex Comfort

BELSHAZZAR AND THE WALL

No desert is as silent as a country
which before any sickness knows itself dead.
I, King Belshazzar, having put down by arms
the enemies of law and order, celebrate
a triumph, making due acknowledgment
to all deities held in honour among us
with public holidays, with games, mock battles,
and every kind of music; carried myself
on four men's shoulders in a gilt chair, followed
by all the prisoners of my liberation
by Freedom and a great noise of chains
into my city in a brass midday
and the skeins of sand follow me through the gate

Having passed through the desert, many valleys alike
lion-faced rocks, lion grass, thirst and barbed plants
my army's tail, a snake, comes through the dust
and it also sings, driving home prisoners.
But all their songs are somehow a part of silence
we have passed through the desert, bringing it with us
clinging to our foot-soles, dust that soaks up all sounds,
sand in the cloth I wear. Water, even the water
is dusty, a stream vanishing into sand,
one moment running, the next a webbed stain.
The bridges in the city span flat dust
A level waterless river floats my ships
All the town streets are jammed with roaring silence

It has been written on a new pillar
it has been made into a durable epic
a pillar of red granite, memorable verses

89

indestructible, hard as Law or Culture
but the characters flow to a dazzle of sand
the readers are bellowing twelve books of silence
a dazzle like imagined desert-water
a silence like the noise of a lion in grass
perhaps from too long looking at the slopes of sand
my soldiers, as they passed through the flagged gate
wondering first, and then uneasy, homeless—
and far back in the column the song died out
until the last rearguard walked in silence

And that day even the clouds had faces
of lions or worn, table-topped rocks or hawks
full of the still dust, their shadows
hung under them, filled hillsides, blotted
the flags and faces, the prisoners' ordered shadows
even the hollow shadows their chains threw
and the sun was large and rusty in that curtain.
They killed a ram under the white lintel
and the King, hoisted out of the gilt seat
by four brown sergeants, lit his butter-lamps
kneeling on a round carpet, grovelling duly—
but from the gods and the people and the brass horns
silence fell heavy as rain, as the shadows of chains.

I am a King. This is a victory. This.
They wait in deference while I thank that image,
thinking a King's high thoughts. Thinking, I cannot get up
because of my belly, unless four men lift me
but kneel here double, as if I were waiting
for my own headsman. I sit bolstered up
on the broad-bottomed pyramid of old,
piled-up kings, perched upon history—
the topmost, balanced, King, keeping my victory—
waiting, like this whole waiting town, that knows itself
too fat in the belly to get off its knees
waiting for an unreal headsman, waiting
under a semblance of giving thanks.

Two hundred gold cups from a previous victory,
much wine in skins, taken from enemies

of freedom, when I last defended it,
together with meat and excellent music, culture
and other things which winning Kings can own.

Two hundred gold cups, the readers of poetry
recounting my own deeds. If I do not look up
above the level of the hangings, up
to the yellow wall, the veined desert stones
for on that sandy table the fine cracks
have the look of pointed writing, meaningless
threatening words. FINISHED. SHORT WEIGHT. STRANGERS.
None of my wise men can interpret them.

Prisoners, like trees in a fruitless orchard
stand in rows swaying with the foodless march
their chains like harness in a dark stable
ringing when one of them moves. Two paces
apart, a desert from their own streets. All
thinking of women whose voices fear curdled
to jackals' voices, three black beams, hot smoke
and similar miles of sand, hear the King scream
a thin yell behind walls, the soldiers drop
their bottle and raise heads to listen. Bright
spearheads lean in rows against the wall.
Silence then, the guard turns back to ease, and they
all equidistant still retread those miles

And in the same night was Belshazzar the king slain,
his throat cut over a basin, cloth
stopping his mouth, his body dumped next day
over the smoking wall. Foreign soldiers drank
the wine. Dignified ministers
carried the stranger's gilt chair on their necks.
The prisoners at morning marched in files
to unfamiliar saltmines having changed masters,
while faces faded dusty in their heads.
But between king and king the silence of dust
broke in one moment's kinglessness. Unsleeping
citizens felt it run, an earthquake shock
before the strangers' knives bloodied their pillows.

91

The houses where they lived are level as the sea
level under a snowfall brown not white
a snowdrift of ashes. All their plots of ground
sown with charcoal and bright blades of glass.
Glass is the children's jewel. Bushes grow.
Stones fall. The branches of columns sing
notes in the wind at night, standing windows
glitter, and in the wind light things travel.
Their clay tablets, and their calendars
their broken pots, knives, children's bones and toys
hollow vessels, seeds, fetters, bottles that held tears.
The sand has grown its beard of thorn-filled plants.
Among them, in their huts, dwell masterless men.

Rainer Maria Rilke

AN OCCURRENCE

(*translated by* Ernst Sigler)

I would be little more than a year ago, when something strange happened to him where the castle-garden falls rather steeply down the slope to the sea. Walking up and down with a book in his hand, as was his custom, it had occurred to him to lean against the shoulder-high fork of a bush-like tree. At once he felt himself so pleasantly supported in this position, and so much at peace, that without reading he remained completely lost in his surroundings, in a state of almost unconscious contemplation. Gradually his attention was aroused by a feeling he had never before known: it was as if from the inside of the tree almost imperceptible vibrations were flowing into him; he easily explained it thus to himself: that a not otherwise visible wind, gliding down flat against the slope, came into its own in the wood—although he had also to admit that the trunk seemed too thick to be so vigorously affected by so slight a breeze. What engaged his thoughts above all, however, was not this or a similar consideration, but he was more and more astonished, deeply stirred even, by the effect this something which ceaselessly surged over into him had produced: gentler movements, he thought, had never filled him; his body, as it were, was treated like a soul and enabled to hold a degree of influence which it really could not have experienced in the normal distinctness of physical conditions. Add to this that he could not immediately identify the sense by which he was receiving so delicate and detailed a communication; also, this condition forming within him was complete and enduring and different from everything else; yet since it was not to be imagined by an intensification of previous experience, he could not, for all its delicacy, call it an enjoyment. All the same, wishing to give an account to himself of especially the gentlest emotion, he asked most urgently what was happening to him, and almost at once found an expression to satisfy him, saying: he had come upon the other side of nature. As sometimes in a dream, this word now gave him joy and he held it to be almost entirely in keeping. Everywhere and with increasing symmetry filled with this force which returned at strangely ardent intervals, his body came to be indescribably pathetic, of use only for standing purely and carefully in him, exactly like a revenant which, residing elsewhere, sadly steps into this once tenderly put-aside something, in order to belong once again, if scattered, to the world formerly held indispensable. Slowly looking about him, though without moving, he recognised everything, remembered it, smiled at it, as it were, with distant affection, let it be—like something which once under different circumstances was a part of him. His eyes followed a bird, a shadow drew his attention, yes, the very path along which he had walked and lost himself filled him with reflective insight which seemed to him the purer since he knew himself to be independent of it. Where else he might be it was beyond him to think, except that he was merely *returning* to all this, that he stood in this body as in the depth of an abandoned window, looking out: of that he was so convinced for a few seconds that the sudden appearance of a dweller in the same house would have staggered him most painfully, while in reality, in his nature, he was prepared to see Polyxene or Raymondine or another dead one of the house step forth from the turning of the way. He comprehended their silent form of supernumerary beings, it was familiar to him to see for a brief moment something of terrestrial shape used in so unconditional a manner; the coherence of their habits suppressed all other education in him; he was certain that moving among them he would not seem extraordinary to them. A vinca growing near him, the blue haze of which he had perhaps met before, now touched him from a more spiritual distance, but with such inexhaustible meaning as if there were no more to be concealed. Altogether he noticed how all objects appeared at one and the same time to be further away and yet somehow more truthful: this might have been due to the look of his eyes which was no longer directed straight in front of him to narrow down, there, in the open: he glanced, as it were, over his shoulder back at things; and added to their—for him—secluded existence was a brave, sweet flavour, as if everything were suddenly seasoned by the flower of farewell. —Though he told himself from time to time that this could not last, he was not afraid of the ending of this extraordinary condition: like music, he felt, it could only come to an infinitely ordered conclusion.

Suddenly his position began to inconvenience him, he became aware of the tree-trunk, the tiredness of the book in his hand, and stepped aside. A breeze turned the leaves in the tree now, it came from the sea; the bushes growing on the slope stirred each other into life.

Robert Payne

FISHING

THE fisherman's boy at dusk lowered his net and gazed out at the swift-flowing river. The sun had set over the gorges, but a frail light still shone on the river, where there were whirlpools and high ragged rocks, and all of them were steel-blue in this light. In the small village among the cliffs small lamps were burning, but their frail light hardly penetrated the evening gloom.

As it grew darker the boy peered over the ledge of rock until he was in danger of falling. He could see the little cork floats bobbing up and down, and he heard the sucking of the water against the rock. Lights flickered on the surface like the saliva of serpents. The darkness was so thick that he could not see distinctly the other side of the river. Sometimes, but they were very rare now, gigantic granite shadows passed downstream, and there were red fires glowing in the well-decks of huge sampans. Along the beach boats were moored, resembling the dead bones of prehistoric animals. A stiff wind came from the direction of the gorges, and now there was no light at all in the sky.

The boy remained huddled on the rock with his back to the wind. He did not know how long he had been there, and he was already hungry. He wore long blue trousers rolled up to his knees, his feet were bare and his thin blue coat had lost the hooks of corded silk which bound it together. Now, as the wind rose, the coat flapped violently, and he would bring his slender shoulder-blades nearer together, as though he could find some comfort in their protection. And all the while his eyes were fixed on the bobbing floats.

He could feel the fish wandering about in the net which was only a few feet under water. Sometimes he could see their silver bodies gleaming faintly in the black water, and once when a huge-masted sampan passed with a fire smouldering in the well-deck, a fire which lit the lower sails crimson, he saw the fishes weaving through the dark cords of the net, and perhaps there were eight of them, with bright yellow button eyes, but he did not count them. He wondered where the sampan was going. He could see people walking about on the deck, very dark against the smoking fires, and there was a girl nursing a baby, her full breasts gleaming scarlet. And there were other people, boys in ragged blue coats and old men sucking at barrel-shaped pipes, but what attracted his attention more than anything else was the sound of singing from the boat. It seemed strange to him that people should sing so happily. The half-naked or naked hauliers, with scratched and crusted skins, covered with scars, never sung such songs. They sang in low-pitched tones of complaint, and always they repeated the same words. But in this ship, whose paintwork glowed dully in the light of the charcoal fire on the well-deck, men were singing in pure delight, and sometimes a girl's voice—the voice of the girl who was feeding the baby—rose towards the faint stars. But the ship passed in the night, there was no more light on the fishes swimming about in his net, and the songs of the mariners grew fainter. He watched the ship enviously as it disappeared between the granite walls of the gorges.

The mountains were so high in this part of the world that he had never seen his long shadow stretching out before him. Even in summer the sun set at seven o'clock. It was a bright sun, and the fields shone with a moist green liquid light, but the mountains were oppressive, shutting out the light. The moon would rise later, etching the slopes of the mountains in silver fire; but in this darkness he was perfectly content to dream of the ship and the red fire and the songs coming from the rigging.

The scents of night, of raw fish, of human flesh, of the ebbing river, all these disappeared in the hush that precedes the moonlight: for though there was as yet no light in the sky everything was hushed and expectant.

No more boats had come down the river for some time. The stars began to come out, marching across the deceitful night with no sudden explosions of fire, but slowly lighting up the ribbed shadowy hulks of the boats moored along the shore. Now by the light of the stars he could see the silver fish gleaming, and he could feel them nibbling languidly at his net. There was life in them still, and they would make sudden scurries, whipping up their faint silver tails, dragging themselves round and round the net in a hopeless effort to find the river; and sometimes those sleek silver-yellow bodies would nuzzle together for comfort, and a great pity welled in the boy.

As the moon came out it set light to his snub nose, and his hairless boy's face, which was almost the face of a girl. It etched with silver lines the thin ribs beneath his smooth shoulder-blades and filled the hollow of his eyes with silver. He was like a mask, or like a young god sitting on the edge of the water, so careless of his appearance that his natural beauty cried out for some girl's arms. And all the while he was thinking dreamily of the girl in the well-deck whose red breasts, seen in the light of the charcoal fires, were like a summons or an invitation. But the boat had passed in the night.

The moon came over the mountains in full silver, raining down its sickles and spears along the sheer slopes, a moon so full and splendid and so blinding that he dared not look up. What had been dark before was suddenly made white, with the whiteness of burnt ash, with little flickering purple flames. And for some reason the appearance of the moon wakened the frogs and the cicadas, and sent the fishes thrashing in the nets, and pouring over the boy's damp hair, made it shine like a glory. It was then that I saw him, as I was coming along the pathway from the gorges, and I would have liked him to stay longer, but at that moment he rose, lifted the silver net from the river and walked back slowly across the dunes towards a small house at the bottom of the cliffs. As he walked the water dripped from his net, and I heard him singing.

Seán Jennett

THE NAVVIES

MADMEN in the guise of naked navvies were building a road. We knew they were mad because they made so joyous a racket with their shovels and picks and pneumatic drills and laughed and sang like children. Then, the road they were building was a work of madness. It had corrugations and undulations like a pool among rocks under a waterfall; it was not possible to travel along it any other way than on foot. It was crowded with people, nevertheless, and it seemed that every one of these people had the same ambition, to join the gang at the end and become a navvy. Some, indeed, were so impatient to apply their own methods of road-building that they had brought mattocks and crowbars with them, with which they belaboured the metal of the road as they went. They did not damage it greatly, but occasionally one of them got his crowbar into a chink made by an earlier passenger and broke off a piece of concrete perhaps as large as a shilling. This he carefully turned over, and then he shouted to everyone else to come and see what he had done; but though he adopted the most marvellous postures and tones, few bothered, for they were all busy boasting about their own achievements and abilities. What with the noise of the navvies, the shouting of the people, and the scrawing of innumerable pet animals, there was a tremendous hullaballoo.

When I saw you first on the opposite pavement the road was centuries wide, but when I leaned over and took your hand it narrowed to seconds, and soon there was no interval between us at all.

We looked for a house where we might escape from the insane noise and bustle, but when we found one it was so extremely narrow that it was hard to get into it. When we first saw it the house was newly built, with the rawness of new brick, but when we reached it we found that it was already crumbling. The door opened straight into a room, and inside was a small boy, who told us that his parents were upstairs. We went up into a bedroom and there was the small boy grown into a man and watching an old woman die under a white counterpane. The room was sour with the mingled smell of medicine and flowers and urine and heavy with the drone of prayers. We prayed also and then came sadly away and descended the stairs to the parlour again. Here was the young man, now shrunken and bald and with a thin white beard on his chin; he was dying, with a bottle of whiskey to comfort him. A small boy played with bones in a corner.

You said you would prefer the street to this house, and so we went out, by the door at which we had entered. The house fell in as we left it, and the rumble of falling walls dazed us.

A crowd of people had gathered around something that lay in the carriageway. They stood bareheaded, holding their hats in their hands as though shielding their genitals. We went in among them, and saw a young man who had been the boy who played with bones. He was sprawled among the fallen bricks, moaning in agony. His limbs were torn and broken. As we watched, a lot of little white maggots came through the skin of his face. This made all the on-lookers run away, crying out, and in a short while the maggots had devoured the young man entirely and had them-selves vanished.

The people were still hurrying forward with their in-effectual mattocks and crowbars, but now some of them had other tools, trowels and hods. These people with trowles and hods were mostly in dark clothes, with untidy hair and flowing scarves and gallant hats, but they were flinging off their garments as they ran, desiring the nakedness of the navvies, as though therein lay their power. Because they did not try to uproot the concrete they got on faster than the others who sought to destroy it; but none of them could come up with the navvies. The madmen worked faster than any of the people could run and were by this far away on the horizon.

I think it was now that you began to weep, because you had not forgotten the young man lying among the bricks, but I did not see at first. I was still looking for a place of peace and asylum from the monomania and the hustling of the throng. I saw the birds in the sky. They flew towards the madmen, but like us they had no ambition. They went that way because it was the common way of life to death, it was in the eternal order of things. They were always trying to build nests in the trees and always before they could finish them the trees grew old and rotten and fell down.

We became a pair of hawks, but in a moment, because you were still thinking about the young man and the maggots, I lost you.

I flew on, savage and furious, and when I saw a doe in a meadow I flung upon it to destroy it. It screamed and I saw the maggots coming up at the back of its eyes. As it ran away I saw that it was you, and followed you, and all the time the centuries were widening between us. It was not until we became dragonflies that we were able to join again, and the defeated years floated away like silk-ash on the wind.

We were so fast now that we could overtake the navvies at their work. They laughed at us and wantonly struck at us with their tools. They jeered and sought to destroy us. At the end of ambition we found only insult and cruelty, the bitter reward of ages of desire. I was weary of life and alighted on a rock, and when you came and lay beside me in the sunlight, it seemed to me that this was sweeter than all strife or labour. The gang of navvies moved farther and farther away, and the hastening throngs went past and left us alone. A blackbird that saw us as it swept by sheered away with a chirrup, and the noise of the drills and the voices of the people began to grow dim and the light to fade.

We were left alone on the bare rock. The sun went down and the dark came, with stars cold and beautiful. It was a long time before I knew that we had died.

Michael Ayrton

DESIGN FOR A MASQUE

THE popular conception of the early seventeenth-century English theatre as a cockpit open to the sky where actors in ordinary dress performed without the aid of scenery is accurate enough only of the popular theatre. Concurrently there existed at court the form of spectacular entertainment known as the masque, which for sumptuousness and extravagance of costume, lavishness of scene and ingenuity of mechanical contrivance has never been improved upon, except in that the invention of electric lighting has increased the range of visual possibilities and simplified the mounting of certain effects.

In these court entertainments, fountains, transformations, cataclysms and all kinds of strange and ingenious phenomena were manifest whilst the poetry of Jonson and D'Avenant was spoken by the courtiers, on occasion led by the members of the royal family itself. Allegories of the seasons, the virtues, the muses and the gods played a substantial part in the proceedings, frequently making their entrances in great chariots or descending on clouds from the heavens. The stage directions for these masques make frightening reading to-day, even for the designer or producer working in a fully equipped modern theatre, and the extent to which the fabulous requirements of the authors were met when the masques were first produced will never really be known. The following quotation from the masque contained in Purcell's *Dioclesian* should give some indication of those requirements. The designer is called upon to follow these instructions:

'While a symphony is playing, a machine descends, so large it fills all the space from the frontispiece of the stage to the further end of the house, and fixes itself by two ladders of clouds to the floor. In it are four several stages, representing the Palaces of two Gods and two Goddesses. The first is the Palace of *Flora*: the columns of red and white marble breaking through the clouds; the columns fluted and wreath'd about with all sorts of flowerage, the pedestals and flutings inrich'd with gold. The second is the Palace of the Goddess *Pomona*: the columns of blue marble, wound about with all kinds of fruitage, and inrich'd with gold as the other. The third is the Palace of *Bacchus*: the columns of green marble, wreath'd and inrich'd with gold, with clusters of grapes hanging round them. The last is the Palace of the Sun; it is supported on either side of rows of *termes*, the lower part white marble, the upper part gold. The whole object is terminated with a glowing cloud, on which is a chair of state, all of gold, the Sun breaking through the cloud, and making a glory about it; as this descends, there rises from under the stage a pleasant prospect of a noble garden, consisting of fountains, and orange trees set in large vases; the middle walk leads to a Palace at a great distance. At the same time enter *Silvanus, Bacchus, Flora, Pomona, Gods of the Rivers, Fauns, Nymphs, Heroes, Heroines, Shepherds, Shepherdesses,* the *Graces* and *Pleasures,* with the rest of their followers. The Dancers place themselves on every stage in the machine: the Singers range themselves about the stage.'

Inigo Jones whose reputation as the greatest of all English stage designers was won for him by just such 'costly scenes, machines and clothes' which he designed for the celebrated series of masques by Ben Jonson, learnt his trade in Italy where court spectacles had earlier been furnished forth by such masters as Leonardo da Vinci and Raphael, and where Palladio, Buontalenti and later the Bibiena family laid the foundations of theatrical décor as we know it today. That Jones, with his Italian training was the moving spirit in the 17th century English theatre design is shown by the quality of the many drawings now in the collection of the Duke of Devonshire at Chatsworth, and it was to these drawings that I turned when I was asked by the Covent Garden Opera Trust to undertake the scenery and costumes for Purcell's *Fairy Queen*.

Fairy Queen was originally called an opera and in the seventeenth-century sense of the word, as being a collection of musical works, it is an opera. But in terms of what we now think of as opera or grand opera it is in a far less familiar form than the more famous *Dido and Aeneas*. *Fairy Queen* is in fact, as the critics with a great air of discovery pointed out, more like a review or pantomime than a coherent music drama and as such is the most immediate descendant of the masques for which Jones designed. *Fairy Queen* in fact is an anonymous doggerel adaptation, with additional dialogue and lyrics, of Shakespeare's *A Midsummer Night's Dream* and this dialogue is almost entirely abject, although the lyrics to which Purcell set his songs are not by any means bad.

In the 1946 revival, by the restoration of ungarbled Shakespeare and by dextrous cutting and adapting, the original five acts were reduced to three with each act following a strictly formal pattern. Each act contains a dramatic scene and a separate masque. Thus Act I opens on the quarrel between Oberon and Titania over the possession of the Indian boy. An entr'acte and ballet of birds follows and then Titania calls upon Night and her followers to send her peaceful sleep. The second scene of Act I is therefore a Masque of Night and almost entirely musical. Night, Mystery, Secrecy and Sleep, each attended by dancers, sing their separate songs to lull Titania to rest. At the close of the act Oberon, who has obtained a magic flower from Puck, squeezes the juice into Titania's eyes so that 'be it ounce, or cat, or bear' she shall fall in love with whoever she sees when first she wakes.

Act II introduces the familiar 'rude mechanicals' rehearsing their play in the wood and the translation of Bottom, who wearing his asses head becomes the object of the waking Titania's love. In her desire to entertain him she transforms the scene to an enchanted lake and summons the singers and dancers to stage a Masque of Love; again a musical second scene to the Act. In the third Act Bottom is released from his enchantment, Oberon and Titania are reconciled and the rising sun personified by Phœbus rises to accept the homage of the Seasons, who with their followers form the third masque. The finale is a transformation to a Chinese Garden where Oberon and Titania are married by Hymen. This Chinese finish is no more nor less than the introduction of a topical note and is intended to crown the proceedings with the strange and fabulous world of the East, which towards the end of the seventeenth century was being opened up to trade. The note of 'Chinoiserie' here is

THE FAIRY QUEEN - MASQUE BY HENRY PURCELL
Act I, Scene I

DANCE OF FAIRIES AND SAVAGES

THE FOLLOWERS OF SUMMER BEFORE PHOEBUS

DRAWING FOR SAVAGE

DESIGN FOR 'SUMMER'

THE FAIRY QUEEN. ENTR'ACTE FOR BIRDS, ACT I

interesting since it foreshadows the immense popularity of the cult in the 18th century. The plot is completed very soon after the opening of Act III and two-thirds of the act are musical. The whole entertainment is, to the audience of today, an extravaganza to the music of England's greatest composer. The illogicality of ending Shakespeare's play in China is simply the taste of the period and is after all preferable to the majority of Hollywood's cinematic tampering with classics.

The original designs for *Fairy Queen* do not appear to exist and in spite of the fact that Inigo Jones had been dead for exactly forty years when *Fairy Queen* was first produced in 1693, I thought it advisable to take his drawings as a basis for my own part of the revival in 1946.

The major problem which confronts the designer who is called upon to restage a period extravaganza today is the inevitable change which has taken place in what is visually familiar to the audience. The invention of the film has robbed the stage of so much in the matter of spectacle and has to a great extent rendered stage effects naif which would only half a century ago have seemed magical and breathtaking. What excitement attaches to a transformation scene from a wood near Athens to a Chinese Garden, in an age when the public is used to being transported momentarily from Twickenham to Timbuctoo, from Hanwell to Hollywood and from Pinner to Penang in any newsreel at any local cinema any week? A seventeenth-century audience would have sat goggling happily for five minutes whilst a symphony was played and one beautiful scene laboriously changed to another even more beautiful. Not so the modern spectator who cannot keep his attention from wandering if a change takes more than thirty seconds. Even this thirty-second transformation no longer carried complete conviction for it lacks the specious realism which the smooth cutting of film gives to the wildest visual extravagances. All that the stage designer can do in the matter is to make the change sufficiently ingenious to prevent the audience from being fully aware of what is happening and how. And yet *Fairy Queen* like all such shows relies on such effects and unlike the ordinary pantomime of today must have a dignity and grace compatible with the superb music of Purcell and the poetry of Shakespeare.

The adaptation of costume is another problem of a similar kind. The dances with which *Fairy Queen* is studded would in the 17th century have been very similar to the formal dancing of the ballroom and costumes such as Jones designed would have been entirely suitable. But to eyes familiar with the wide variety of dancing used in modern ballet, these dances would after a short time seem antiquarian and dull. It was therefore rightly decided that the full range of contemporary choreography should be used in the revival and this necessitated costumes which would provide considerable freedom of movement without destroying the sense of period. Where possible in these circumstances I continued to base my designs on the traditional forms, but in numerous cases it was necessary to make a complete departure and rely entirely on my own invention. The costumes for the Spirits of the Air in Act II and for the followers of the Seasons in Act III are cases in point. In actual fact I merely continued the tradition of adapting an entertainment to contemporary taste in much the same way that the author of *Fairy Queen* adapted Shakespeare and, years earlier, Inigo Jones adapted the already much adapted classical conventions of architecture and costume to suit his audience.

The masque is essentially an English phenomenon in spite of its Italian origin and as a form of entertainment it has lived on. Today it appears as ballet and as review, split into sections, but the success of *Fairy Queen* would seem to show that its original portmanteau form, displaying all the arts, is still acceptable. There seems to be no essential reason why contemporary poets, composers and painters should not contrive new masques, not for a court but for the public. It could do much to bridge the gaps between highbrows, lowbrows, balletomanes, music lovers and devotees of the drama. The masque is essentially a lighthearted entertainment most welcome in this bleak age. It is also a great joy for the designer.

Peter Goffin

THE END OF ART

IN the Victorian affection for the sham front and the false
bottom, at which we are so inclined to poke fun, not the
least of the social problems and crises which afflict us
now took shape. For it was in the useful thing made to
look useless, and in the seemingly useless object with a
secret purpose, that the spiritual obliquity and self-deception
of the generation which fathered our own found something
of its material expression. Behind a pretentious façade of
prosperity the social structure we inherited was already
cracked to the very foundations. The crucial industries of
the Church, the Laboratory, and the Studio, flaunting the
names of Religion, Science, and Art (with added capitals,
but deprived of their proper meanings), had established
themselves as independent and inimical concerns. The three
vital organs of the public body, as it were, had severed their
connections and were functioning as private interests: the
lungs only working for self-expansion, the brain with no
thought but for itself, and the heart refusing to circulate the
blood. A rapid decline of the social organism's health was
inevitable.

Although the terminology differed in each case, the three
concerns preached and practised the same doctrine. The
Church called it Salvation; the Laboratory, Progress; and
the Studio, Art for Art's sake. This doctrine, still popular
despite its pernicious consequences, is based on the supposition that Art and Life stand diametrically opposed to one
another. Accordingly, the artist is an extraordinary being,
superhuman or subhuman, angel or fool, whose inexplicable
activity is not of this utilitarian world.

The traditional conception of art, which this nineteenth-
century doctrine usurped, held that art embraces all making,
and that all human beings are artists of some sort. From this

standpoint, the notion of art as a separate profession was inconceivable. Indeed, there was no special thing called art, it was simply the human way of working as distinct from the way of nature. 'If anyone was called a master of arts it was', as Eric Gill reminds us, 'one who had mastered the humanities; and this may still be seen by the title given to persons who, in those medieval institutions called universities, have passed more or less successfully through a course of studies in human language, philosophy or divinity.'

It is true, of course, that the traditional conception began to fall from favour centuries before the Victorians finally dropped it; but there can be no doubt that it was the peculiar achievement of the nineteenth century to substitute an arbitrary distinction of class for the natural one of function between painters and engineers, or between those who write poems and those who print them. This arbitrary division of human labour and the distortion of human values which it carries with it is what chiefly concerns me here, but it is far from my intention to argue that there is no distinction to be drawn between those arts which are now called 'fine' and other kinds of human skill.

The definition of art as skill is too simple. A man cannot have skill alone, for nature gave all men imagination, sensibility and intelligence—however the nurture to which we are subjected in our upbringing and education may upset the disposition of these faculties and impede their growth. Hence the difference between one work of art and another is never purely a matter of more or less skill. In highly mechanised work, of course, precious little of anything but skill is required. When just enough of it has been acquired to perform the prescribed task, the worker's action may become almost as mechanical as that of a machine, but never wholly so, for a machine is a product of art, a thing—whereas a man is a product of nature, however he may try to ignore the fact.

Moreover, when we come to the distinction between 'fine' and other kinds of art the presence of differences other than those of skill becomes obvious, even between works considered to be of the same kind. Consider, for instance, two familiar paintings: El Greco's *Agony in the Garden*, and Holman Hunt's *Light of the World*. In what is popularly called the 'subject', these pictures are similar; that is to say, they are both pictures of Jesus Christ. It is also evident that both of them were painted with considerable skill. We do not question the painters' workmanship. And yet I would go so far as to say that there is an essential difference between these paintings at least as great as that which separates Shakespeare's *Hamlet* from a Chippendale chair; and I will confess at once that it is not the El Greco that I would classify as furniture.

But what is this essential difference? Picasso provides more than a hint of the answer in his saying: 'There are painters who transform the sun into a yellow spot, but there are others who, thanks to their art and intelligence, transform a yellow spot into the sun'. In the particular case we are considering the light of the world is not the sun but the Son of God; and I would say that Holman Hunt, as he effected the transformation of this radiance, qualified himself for Picasso's first category of painters, and El Greco, as he effected it, for the second. The essential difference between the paintings lies in the kind and quality of the painter's vision. 'What, it will be Question'd, When the Sun rises, do you not see a round disc of fire somewhat like a Guinea? O no, no, I see an Innumerable company of the Heavenly host crying, Holy, Holy, Holy is the Lord God Almighty. I question not my Corporeal or Vegetative Eye any more than I would question a Window concerning a Sight. I look thro' it & not with it.'

When a man gives expression to his vision in words or by other means of art, he is bound to make use of a language of signs and symbols. Simply as a reporter of what he sees with what Blake calls his Corporeal or Vegetative Eye, he will use the familiar conventional signs that are commonly understood to signify or 'represent' the objects of the visible and tangible world. In this case, if he happens to be a painter, he will endeavour to make an image of a rose that will yield sensations to the spectator as nearly as possible identical with those evoked by the rose itself. It will be a representative image made only for the physical eye.

But in addition to this photographic vision, man is capable of insight. Not only can he see roses in summer when they are in flower before him, but in winter when there are no roses; and if he would express his vision of flowers that grow only in the realm of imagination he will use, not only the factual sign-language of the reporter, but the symbolic language of the poet. It is not the function of the man of poetic vision to report, but to create. His works come, not from the outer world of popular dimensions, but out from the incalculable and unique inner world of his own soul.

These different functions of 'fine' art, no less than those of other kinds of work, form the basis of the natural division of human labour; and the traditional view of art recognised that what is natural in man cannot be ignored with impunity. The Victorians, however, thought otherwise. With the apotheosis of Capitalism, under a dense cloud of heavy industrial smoke, an arbitrary distinction of class was substituted for the natural one of function and capacity. The growth of Capitalism was, as John Dewey has pointed out, 'a powerful influence in the development of the museum as the proper home for works of art, and in the promotion of the idea that they are apart from the common life. The *nouveaux riches*, who are an important by-product of the capitalist system, have felt especially bound to surround themselves with works of fine art which, being rare, are also costly. Generally speaking, the typical collector is the typical capitalist. For evidence of good standing in the realm of higher culture, he amasses paintings, statuary, and artistic *bijoux*, as his stocks and bonds certify to his standing in the economic world'.[1]

Since the narrow æstheticism of the art for art's sake doctrine excludes from the realm of art all work but that of the painter, poet, and sculptor, I would wish to see it discarded, not more for the sake of the numerous and anonymous makers of everyday things than for the few who compose poems or carve stone, but because we cannot live without the spiritual values of art, nor can we live well while these values are divorced from the common work of daily life. The evidence against the division is before us: on the one hand, the 'artist' whose sole concern is self-expression, and on the other, the unit of manpower with no self to express.

The faculties of our nature are divisible only in theory;

1 *Art as Experience*, London, 1934.

in the life-process they are interdependent and indivisible. The gravest mistake we can make is to assume that the problems arising with the growth and development of social life require only a material, only a mental, or only a spiritual solution; and to act accordingly. And yet, as may be seen, it is just this dangerous misconception that we do act upon; for we have segregated and falsified the love that is the creative principle of religion, the knowledge that is truly science, and the faculty of skill which underlies all our making.

In the traditional sense, the capacity for art is a biological factor in human life; and, as Aristotle expresses it, the general end of art is the good of man. In this sense, all that is implied by science and religion is involved in the processes of art. If by science we mean knowledge of the materials and workings of nature, and the organisation of an intellectual relationship to the world we live in; and if by religion we mean the relationship of the self to the not-self, of the individual to the whole in harmony or love; then the opposition that is supposed to exist between religion and science is not of these at all, but of incompatible creeds or ideologies which have taken their names. Nevertheless, as things are, the opposition remains. Nor is it to be resolved merely by changing the names of the contending parties. Moreover, the supposition that the general end of art is the good of man omits the hazard of the individual human will: of choice. Nature gave trunks to elephants, and we can but suppose that the general end for which they were provided was to provide for the good of the species. But if an elephant so willed it, he might use his trunk to strangle another elephant, even to choke himself. Animals, however, live artlessly.

At the beginning, no doubt, the capacity for art in man, like the elephant's trunk, greatly added to the creature's natural or instinctive means of fulfilling primary physiological requirements, and of adjusting himself to his environment; but it brought with it needs of a very different and more subtle order: the needs of the self-conscious spirit and reflective mind. The primary rhythms of animal life persist in man and become conscious with him. Out of his experience and knowledge of them he formulates meaning and purpose.

III

At the primitive level of human life, as we know from the findings of anthropologists, art and nature interact harmoniously, and the several branches of art work together as members of one another; for primitive man is at once mystic, scientist, and poet. He is not more concerned to gain knowledge of natural processes than to achieve the conquest of his own soul, and the skill with which he cultivates the earth is valued neither more nor less than that with which he celebrates in painting, song, and dance the Great Magical Spirit whose awe-inspiring work is everywhere about. In the beginning, the end of art was prefigured in the act of living, in the daily fulfilment of the needs of body and soul, in sorrow and joy.

The theory of the traditional conception of art (Asiatic and European) is an intellectual formulation of the primitive mode. 'Life itself—', writes Ananda Coomaraswamy, 'the different ways in which the difficult problems of human association have been solved—represents the ultimate and chief of the arts of Asia; and it must be stated once for all that the forms assumed by this life are by no means empirically determined, but designed as far as possible according to a metaphysical tradition, on the one hand conformably to a divine order, and on the other with a view to facilitating the attainment by each individual of approximate perfection in his kind, that is, permitting him, by an exact adjustment of opportunity to potentiality, to achieve such realisation of his entire being as is possible to him.'[2]

Thus, whatever the work a man may do, it is so performed that its close is a consummation: at one and the same time an objective and subjective satisfaction and delight. It is an act of creation and recreation, of love—not only of the body, but of mind and spirit—a truly æsthetic experience. So it is, in the traditional view, as expressed by Eckhart, 'that man prepares all things to return to God, in so far as he sees them intellectually and not merely sensibly'. This is the meaning or end of art.

A common objection is made, somewhat obviously, to the effect that modern man does not live at the primitive level, nor in a medieval community. Things are quite different

2 Ananda Coomaraswamy: *Transformation of Nature in Art*. Harvard University Press, 1934.

now. Yes, indeed, *things* are quite different—the things which man has made, and with which he has engulfed himself. With prodigious skill and industry he has made the world practically impossible to live in. But what of our selves? Are we so changed in essence? Evidently not, for we cannot adjust ourselves to the circumstances we have made. Under the hard and brittle veneer of our vaunted civilisation we have imprisoned and thwarted our primitive instincts and desires, our humanity. And we are at the bursting point.

'Before the introduction or invention of language,' writes Dr. Burrow, 'of socially agreed signs and symbols, or before the adoption of man of the projective, intellectual mechanism of attention as we now know it, the organism's adjustment to its surroundings was affected, as we know, by means of certain general tensional alternations. These reactions constituted an integral, a systematic or an organic mode of adaption or attention. Through this process of attention the organism as a whole encountered its environment as a whole . . . In response to this integral species of attention the organism performed its various 'instinctive' functions . . . By virtue of these functions, alternately cumulative and dissipatory, the animal procured its food, gathered for the winter, sought shelter, found repose, grew tense or relaxed, slept or awakened. There was thus maintained that physiological balance of tensions and releases through which the total organism secured its internal adjustment to external conditions.'

And there can be no doubt of the fact that 'these internal tensions constituted for man, as for the lower orders of animals, a medium of inter-individual communication as comprehensive and as efficient for the purpose of the organism as a whole as the sophisticated symbols of interchange that have come to serve the purpose of man in his social inter-communication today.'[3]

It is clear, then, that if the purposes for which man exercises his capacity for art over and above those which enable him to maintain the vital physiological balance of his animal nature actually upset that balance and frustrate that nature, such purposes can only be regarded as anti-life and anti-social purposes. Art turned against itself, defeating its own end.

[3] Trigant Burrow: *The Structure of Insanity*, London, 1932.

'The damned-up instinct-forces in civilised man are immensely more destructive, and hence more dangerous, than the instincts of the primitive, who in a modest degree is constantly living his negative instincts. Consequently no war of the historical past can rival a war between civilised nations in its colossal scale of horror.'[4]

And war is a work of art in which every kind of skill is conscripted. Here, all the branches of art are made to work together in diabolical harmony. Under State control the crucial industries of Church, Laboratory, and Studio sink their differences in the common cause. The clergy bless and sanction the conversion of plough, hammer, and sickle into engines of death; and find moral justifications for sending their own congregations to slaughter and to be slaughtered. The scientists find new and ingenious means of increasing the slaughter in magnitude and cruelty. And the 'artists', in official uniform, are commissioned to record the most spectacular scenes of destruction in paint, or to glorify brutality in verse. The end of art is here the annihilation of man. The logical outcome of the doctrine: Art for Art's sake.

And yet not all men and women are willing to be conscripted. Some object, and cannot be forced. They will object as they have always objected, not by opposing violence with violence or by resisting evil, but by affirming their belief in the individual human person as a creature of free will and untold possibilities, and in the spiritual equality of all men. Nor will they formulate their belief as a doctrine. They will show it in being and in works, in love and understanding expressed in the things they make and do. They will be the artists who remain faithful to what Alexander Blok called The Spirit of Music—the underlying harmony of organic life. And their art, whatever form it may take, will express the joy of being oneself, of living, and of human fellowship. Society may crucify them, but their power no power on earth can destroy.

The choice rests with each one of us. In proportion as the number of objectors increases, the object of objection will diminish. We shall make life the end of art only when we cease to end life by the means of art.

[4] C. G. Jung: *Psychological Types*, London, 1938.

Peter Vansittart

AN INTRODUCTION
TO THE FOOL

HISTORICAL cycles at least repeat themselves in-
somuch that they all record the slow growth of
totalitarianism, the decay of public creativity and
individual self-consciousness. Modern Europe
differs only in technique and degree from the hysterical ferment of corrupted power in which Rome and Byzantium
had collapsed. Shooting, as Lewis Mumford remarks,
simplified the art of government and at no time since the
rise of metallurgy have populations been so subjected and
obsessed, anticipated though our present dilemma has been
by the social paralysis of the Fall of Rome and by that
annihilation of the ideal of Total Man covered by the
Reformation.

Within the microcosm of Drama the role of Fool expands
in proportion to social despotism. The spontaneous French
reaction to the sixteenth-century promise of royal abso-
lutism was, for instance, the formation of Fool Societies to
ridicule authority and respectability, ideals of the static
societies which it is the nature of despotisms to demand.
These were modelled on the Danse Macabre which aimed to
exorcise Plague by impersonating and mocking Death in the
manner of forgotten primitives whose ritual and legend,
despite the elaborate façades of civilisation, still survived
and even conditioned religious and monarchical societies.
Primitives had deliberately deified the spirit of disrespect to
avoid the consequences of power and variety which, in the
Theseus myth, arouses anger and retribution from the Gods.
Our habit of touching wood after a boast is an inheritance
from the rite to placate the lurking tree-spirit jealous of the
pretensions of man. Fools, generally drunkards, cripples,

lunatics or poets, sharing abnormalities then considered divine, had the function of satirising and purifying individual and institutions, a custom which endured until the recent times in public saturnalias and carnivals, and in the private jester who, as confessor, wit, medium, pimp and seer, compensated the monotonous and artificial households of over-dominant classes and which, in the decay of the *ancien régime*, sustained themselves by intrigue, eroticism, masochism and murderous practical jokes. The increasing organisation required by the Metal Age was to cause further mental complexes and practical problems whose solutions entailed rituals, the founders and protagonists of which became gods. Ritual procedure for propitiation and mutual benefit was recollected in myths reflecting social and psychological processes, the more fantastic and inconsistent the myth the greater the social challenges and neurosis. As messenger, buffoon and bawd the Fool, like the Elizabethan clown, had the important part of linking authority with submission, heaven with earth, profundity with ribaldry, completing the necessary harmony, and, when the perfection of ritual established regular Drama, linking gods and men, Hero and audience. In times of stress the Fool retained his earlier social function of scapegoat, through whom disease and evil were ceremoniously exiled. The custom of the Fool impersonating the king and being publicly maltreated to prevent extravagant faith in human authority echoes the bloodier rite in which a pure, that is, an exceptional substitute beloved of heaven, was sacrificed on behalf of the Divine King whose ritual murder survived in varying forms into medievalism. It is apparent not only in the Christian sacraments and in the set-up of the Mystery and Morality Plays but also in the untimely deaths of such rulers as Arthur and Barbarossa which Christians and pagans alike seem to have regarded as the sacrifice requisite for social preservation and development, entailing prophetic legends of resurrection and return. In Greek, Celtic, Scandinavian and Oriental mythologies which supplied glossaries not only for the lay Drama but to the Mass, the greatest Drama of all, the Fool, as Hermes, Percival, Loki, Vidusaka, Satan, relieved the tension with obscenity, mirth and irreverence, drew the themes together and prevented social and intellectual atrophy in Life and Drama, both of which were always in danger of becoming over-stylised and esoteric. Simultaneously commercialism, needing disciplined and specialised labour and military groups, provoked, by its standardisation of slavery and caste, a desire for the Fool as Mediator and Saviour, in religion and also in Drama, which, in the public theatre and private Mysteries, was the civic interpreter of religion. Caste states demanded much political and sexual repression, the rulers, becoming more sensitive to criticism, increasing their yoke from which individuals could find only emotional relief, by insulting and abusing the ruler through parodying Fools or through tales of Fools disguised as kings. The unusual names of Fools, Rumpelstiltskin is one, were required by the old tabus against mentioning the actual name of the god or king, the discovery and utterance of which was thought likely to lead to cosmic disturbances and to the castration or impotence of the possessor. Certain sexual activities, metaphors, oaths and dances, were suppressed and, driven into the unconscious, reappeared in artistic symbolism, and in pornographic fairy-tales and mimes of wine-gods, adulterers and panders through which senses could still be titillated and impulses expressed while in a Tom Thumb or Goody Two Shoes a sexual freedom could be preserved at second-hand. The original psychological freedom makes surviving primitive societies absorbing and instructive to modern psychologists and educationalists. The Drama Fool, as Son-God, Youngest Son, or Hero's licensed aide, comforted the populace by mocking such authoritarian figures as Zeus and Agamemnon while, in general mythology, the gods of defeated cities would become devil and clown divinities, mischievous and treacherous, upon whom enslaved and anxious subjects of an expanding or transitional State could hang their desires and prejudices. Similarly, fertility or clown-gods like Robin Hood and his Russian and Tartar equivalents, evolved into quasi-historical figures of national liberation. With the eventual failure of the régime, for aggression denotes inward decay, these deities might enjoy resurrection as Messiahs and Peaceful Gods to whom the great Power-Gods must in turn submit. Though Western Christianity soon theologised Christ into the traditional pattern of the Dying

God, or scapegoat, there survived a primitive Christianity in the Nestorian, Gnostic and Provençal heresies which combined a mystical and Oriental conception of baptism and after-life with a practical belief in fraternity, poverty and self-sacrifice centring round the Synoptic Christ whose paradoxical utterances, disconcerting gentleness and uncompromising distrust of outward appearances are attributes of the Fool at his most sublime.

Disguised as religious and heretical cults, secret societies denounced authority and tried to mitigate it by ancient techniques of magic in which the Fool, the Rare One, the Rejected, had a leading part. In literature he appears as the astute but superficially simple peasant, the Booby or Hans in Luck whose directness continually traps and ridicules the great ones. The Norse Gudbrand modernises the wise-simpleton in a theme whose roots are universal. The ballad of King John and the Abbot, of Peasant Mardok who outwitted Solomon, of Foolish Ivan who won the Tsar's Daughter, all instance both an intellectual defence-symbol of the dispossessed and a sublimation of the guilt feelings of unbalanced and tyrannical societies.

The impoverishment of Rome meant that civilised society had very largely to begin afresh, with medievalism as its creative and imperialism as its destructive and internecine stage, a formula which no civilisation has apparently been able to transcend. The Fool remained, at first relatively normal, as Vice, Saint and Devil in popular drama, his cowl, coxcomb and bells, or horns and tail substantiating his primitive origin as remnants of a disguise for ritual combat or sacrifice. (Private households retained the Jester until the seventeenth century when social dissensions threw up such new forms of expression and relief as the novel and opera and such wider symbols as the Nation and Flag. The power of the royal and ecclesiastical jesters had been considerable even in political affairs, nor was this thought abnormal.) But by the fourteenth century, the age of the Decameron, the social groupings that by balancing each other had produced the creative tension requisite for memorable co-operative enterprises were in collision or disintegration. Crusade, plague, commerce, and the inability of such institutions as the Papacy and Guilds to withstand the temptations of material power had destroyed the promise of the great twelfth century. Threatened, Catholicism returned to the persecution of nonconformists while the kings and traders, capitalising the centralising tendencies of decay, set in motion absolute monarchies, exterminating or emasculating classes now anti-social: monks, knights, witches. The appearance, in rhyme, wood-cut, and drama, of Don Juan, Scaramouch, and Eulenspiegel, was the protest against the new authoritarianism, idealising an earlier, more varied and improvised régime of mirth and horseplay. After the Religious Wars the saturnalia, holy-days and militant heresies were eliminated and thus, in the world of thought and fantasy, the more vivid and poignant grew the Fool-images of defiance, perfidy and disrespect: Thersites, Punch, Falstaff, through whose shrewd simplicity the conventions of the police-state could be partially evaded. What the amoral and irrepressible Punch expressed for the mob in pantomime and puppet-show was repeated by Don Juan and Figaro, both for the revolutionary bourgeoisie and also for the nobility which delighted to mock and torture itself out of an apathetic sophistication due to its political insulation and its failure to escape the formalities and morbid etiquette that had driven its younger scions to obscurantism, eccentricity or revolutionary activity. The cry for relief and salvation from over-centralised, under-nourished states insufficiently appeased by bourgeois Romanticism and political revolution, deepened with the gathering neurosis. Rulers themselves were often as disillusioned as the dispossessed and even the great revolution stopped short with a shoddy Napoleon. Each class explored its own Fool myth. It is a commonplace that, in an earlier generation, Lear's passage from authority to madness showed him the fundamental reality, the dissolution of the illusion of temporal power which the poetic simplicity of his own fool had known throughout. This theme of redemption through suffering shown in the Theseus cycle becomes history in the progress towards disillusionment of such rulers as Boris Godounov and Ivan the Terrible, together with the desire for the higher Fool of a Ludwig II or a Nicholas II who found in Wagner and Rasputin the qualities, half mystical, half mendacious which compensated their own fatalism or disgust with political opportunism and corruption. Similarly, the French and German bourgeoisie demanded and gave itself to the mysterious and unpredictable Napoleon III and Hitler, while Anglo-Saxon cities shed some of their frustrations, boredoms and repressions in the scapegoat pathos of a Chaplin and the iconoclasm of a Groucho Marx. These figures shared a direct and intuitive approach to physical and psychological problems which, at the crisis of capitalist development seemed no longer soluble by the intellect. The whole latter tendency has been away from reason and personal responsibility and towards the archaic pattern of sin, saviour and sacrifice. The comparative failure of industrialism caused a guilt-feeling that the wars and bank-ruptcies were due to sin and this, together with military defeat and the decline of the after-life belief provided the general need for the Dictator, the extreme limit of the Hero, or perverted Fool. Opposing him is the Divine Fool, the eternal antagonist whose simplicity, love and suffering are incarnate in the gentle but persistent figures of Lao Tsu, Don Quixote, the Idiot, the Young Baron, and even perhaps in Luther and Lenin who, despite moral and philosophical dissimilarities knew, like them, that only through utter social and mental revolution, revaluation and austerity could society be repaired and reunited. In the art of a Picasso, Rouault, Daskal, it is not astonishing to find again and again the equivocal Fool hovering like a naked mark of interrogation at the back of a society which maintains the forms but dis-cards the facts of rational and compassionate behaviour. Of the younger painters Cecil Collins in particular has shown, in some remarkable drawings and paintings, the inner con-sistency beneath the apparent irrelevancies and disjointed-ness of the Fool, deriding superficial notions of progress and vitality.

MOTHER AND CHILD
Oil Painting by Mervyn Peake

THE SHEPHERD FOOL
Watercolour by Cecil Collins

JUDITH HOLMANN
by Lawrence Girving

THE ROAD TO THE SEA

Gouache by John Minton

Bernard Denvir

THE RENAISSANCE OF THE SYMBOL

THE expectant world which attended the detonation of the atom bomb in the South Pacific was assisting at a sacrament of history, an outward sign of the inward grace of time. Materialised in the all too beautiful design of disintegrating matter was the spirit of the age. The long slow climb of European empiricism had reached its peak, only to discover further heights, and the range of more distant horizons. The scientist has been within a hair's breadth of grasping in his hand the world of reality, and now it has slipped away, like sand through his fingers, no more tenable than the anthropomorphic fancies of the mythologies, or the syllogisms of the school-men. Once that the certainties of the Aristotelian system had dissolved in a cloud of humiliating negation, the civilised mind was as undefended as Lazarus, and like that earlier revenant, sought again with hysterical fervour the stable certainty of the tomb.

The position of the artist in this maelstrom of exploration is an equivocal one, complicated by the *ignis fatuus* of the pictorial absolute. The classical-romantic antithesis in art and literature is parallel to the male and female one in the world of emotion and feeling. In painting it is revealed in the division between those who extract their forms from nature, and those who impose them on it; nature, in this context being taken to mean, as perhaps it always should in æsthetic discussion, the whole world of the inanimate *id*. Between that simple contrast and the actual interpretation put on it, however, a whole host of complicating factors intervene; emotional patterns, national characteristics and historical context, all conspire to give what is no more than a contemporary mode of vision the fascinating finality of the absolute. The visual world of primitive man revolves around concepts which are strange and alien to us, but to him they are statements of incontroversial fact, and any other mode of expression would be the wildest affectation, divorced from any reality. The grand-daughter of Holman-Hunt in condemning the work of Picasso was not formulating a judgment of two art forms; she was confounding a subjective reality with an objective illusion.

History may well be defined as the imposition of a pattern upon time; plastic art as the imposition of a pattern on the world of appearance; both imply a principle of selection. We have long been prone to accept the idea of selectivity as a second best approach to reality, basing our contempt for it on the claims made by the scientist to a superhuman objectivity. The scientist is now constrained to place an increasing emphasis on the ultimate safety of formula, and has created a vocabulary of thought as abstract as that of any Neo-platonist.

The antithesis between the semi-subjective and the semi-objective approach is one which is very clearly revealed in modern British painting, though its clarity is probably more obvious to the critic of today than it will be to the historian of tomorrow. The difference between the work of a Pasmore or a Gowing, and that of a Minton or an Ayrton is really no more profound than that between the work of Leonardo and Crivelli, and these two were contemporaries in the fifteenth century.

The 'non-abstract' painters chose their symbols from amongst the customary things of life. Their choice is selective rather than creative, and rests for its ultimate success, not upon the passivity of the spectator, but upon his active co-operation. The pink rose in the milky glass, the rotund apple rich in its painterly self-satisfaction, the delicate tendrils of a pastoral scene, invite a conspiracy of taste, a pact of sensitivity. It is not without its significance that most of the Euston Road School painters passed through an earlier, abstract period, and that Graham Bell, their apologist, evolved a series of æsthetic principles based on the idea of an evolution through Picasso.

The painter of the still-life, the commentator on the minutiæ of social existence, is constrained to extract his deeper significances from an attention to the skill of his craft. The secret of the Chardins of this world is that they reach the self-forgetfulness of prophetic intensity through absorption in technique. Matter to them is a by-product of form. To a certain extent this is away from the native tradition; Turner and Constable succeeded because they achieved a tension between what they wanted to say and how they said it, and the most usual accusation levelled against the latter is the same as that most commonly directed against Picasso, that his 'message' has stepped outside the legitimate boundaries of painting. The more usual English preoccupation is what has come to be called a 'literary' one, though to use that epithet in an inevitably derogatory sense is both unjust and illogical. In rekindling the flames of English 'Romanticism' the young painters of today are not being revivalists so much as traditionalists, who are fortunate in finding in their private inheritance a line of development which dovetails into the exact spot where the School of Paris has left the main European growth.

The war has been as a catalyst to British painting. It was not merely the sense of isolation from the Continent, the new economic stimulus, the sympathy and interest of a public gradually becoming more 'culture-conscious'; these were but the earths; the flash of inspiration from Olympus was the agitation of instinct which is the necessary concomitant of war. The older generation had gone through the fires of surrealism and excessive abstraction; John Piper, Cecil Collins, Paul Nash and Julian Trevelyan had all tampered with the flesh-pots of intellectual self-consciousness, but their tampering lacked the dialectical enthusiasm of their continental counterparts. It was a stage in their growth, rather than an ultimate goal of achievement. Surrealism, after all, meant no more than a renewal of the emphasis on subject-matter and content, but whereas the Dalis had to shark up a tradition from the forgotten lumber rooms of European painting, the English artist had to do little more than give freer rein to his own instincts. Blake, Palmer, Calvert and Martin were all, in their different ways, close to a line of continuous craftsmanship. The excessive professionalism which in France had been initiated by the state control of art under Le Brun and continued in the traditions of the Academy had stifled the sources of purely poetic inspiration. Despite the work of Walter Greaves and Alfred Wallis, England never had need of a Douanier Rousseau to establish contact with a more instinctive form of painting. Blake in the nineteenth century was consciously as well as instinctively inspired by the work of the Winchester artists. (*Note.* Anthony Blunt in an illuminating essay on *Blake's Pictorial Imagination*, reprinted in *England and the Mediterranean Tradition*', Oxford 1945, has traced the sources of Blake's imagery), and today it is possible to underline the Celtic, calligraphic element which predominates in the work of men like David Jones, Ceri Richards, and, to a certain extent, Cecil Collins.

Any emphasis on content is bound, in 1948, to lead to a quest for a symbolism which will at once express the artistic personality of the individual and be sufficiently broad in its comprehensiveness to conform to a fairly generalised level of understanding. Sir Kenneth Clark has pointed out (*The Gothic Revival*, London, 1928, pp 207-208) the connexion between the religious formalism of the Gothic revival, the ecclesiological preoccupations of the Camden Society, and the achievement by symbolism of the sudden popularity of a new sport. The mid-nineteenth century may indeed be taken as a convenient starting point of that new interest in significant content, as opposed to significant form, which today has reached a new level of intensity in the iconographical researches of the art-scholar and the plastic experiments of the artist.

The realisation that the explorations of the historian are mirrored in the activity of the artist is a stimulating one. No one who is interested in contemporary painting can have failed to notice the formal identity which links so many personal universes of vision. The significance of colourranges is one which has not yet been fully explored. It is, for instance, a matter of some sociological interest that an age which saw the rediscovery of El Greco has now come to apply to clothes and to the whole range of domestic art just those combinations of purple, sulphurous yellow and mustard green which were used by the Master of Toledo. There may be something to be said for the theory that a predominantly blue tonality is indicative of a youthful stage in an artist's growth. It is to be found at any rate in a good deal of the work of John Craxton, Michael Ayrton, John Minton, Keith Vaughan and Leslie Hurry, as well as being connected with the early paintings of Picasso. On the other hand there is a case to be made out for its being the *couleur de siècle*; blue has become synonymous with the whole range of urban neuroses.

The identity of imagery which, with variations of personality, is sought for by the younger artists is one which endeavours in formal relations to find an order for and a metaphor of the relationship between man and his universe. The difficulty of course is to reconcile the esoteric nuances of personal experience with a very real need of establishing contact with the generality of human understanding. Two great systems, classical mythology and Christian iconography, have broken down, and are of value only when used in a sense different to their original one, whilst the attempt to make the imagery of the subconscious a vehicle of universal understanding was only a partial success.

The characterisation of natural forms and the desire to link them with humanity has a longer history than that of landscape painting, in the limited meaning we have come to attribute to that phrase since the time of Titian and Rubens. Even at his most assertive the English painter will use nature as a repertory of images, the French as one of similies and the tendency today is still to submit passively to the spell of phenomena rather than to assert a dominion of intellect. The only difference between the Euston Road School and the Romantics in this respect is that the one sees the world in significant detail, the other under the guise of the imaginary unity which is concealed at the heart of a proliferating multiplicity of form.

The dry, acid undertones of Graham Sutherland's excursions into the structure of the world reveal his preoccupation with the visible universe as an extension of the imagination, which is moulded by what it embodies. The intuitive flame of comprehension which burns in his work has been an influence of paramount importance on the younger generation, and it is interesting therefore to find, in his own words, a rough guide to the workings of his artistic personality.

'About my thorn pictures; I can only give a clue, since the process of becoming involved with one's subject is always mysterious and not easy to explain. One reacts to the reality of tension in a subject, physical and spiritual or psychological; and that tension, paraphrased and ordered, should become intensified in one's paintings. I had been thinking of the Crucifixion (as you know I hope to attempt this subject for St. Matthew, Northampton); my mind became preoccupied with the idea of thorns (the crown of thorns) and wounds made by thorns. Then, on going into the country, I began to notice thorn trees and bushes. Especially against the sky, the thorns on the branches established a sort of aerial space. They were like dividers, pricking out points in space in all directions, encompassing the air, as if it were solid and tangible. I'd never noticed this before; but all kinds of ideas for pictures started to come into my mind. Apart from the large 'thorn trees' I had all sorts of ideas for 'Thorn Heads'. A sort of 'pricking' and demarcation of a hollow, head-shaped space, enclosed by the points. All the paintings I have done started off with drawings and sketches direct from nature.' (Letter to Curt Valentin, in *Catalogue of Exhibition*, Bucholz Gallery, New York, 1946.)

If there is in fact a revival of English painting, Sutherland is one of the primitives of the school; his work has a vehemence and a cogency which strike a new note. That is the point at which the 'romantics' are more exposed than their Impressionist colleagues; in not leaning so heavily on the prop of taste, they expose themselves to the risks of apparent vulgarity. It is hard to say when vehemence becomes hysteria, and even an artist like Rowlandson was forced by the intensity of his feeling to a mood approaching incoherence. The emotional vigour of Mervyn Peake's illustrations, and the gigantic crescendo of Francis Bacon's assaults on the mind and feeling of the spectator show that the strength and the weakness of passion in art occur at the same point. Bacon is exceptional in being essentially a painter in oils. The spontaneity of the romantic impression has always demanded a more instantaneous medium, and one of the major problems of today is the opposition of a desire for *les grandes machines*, coupled with a weakness for water colour, gouache and pen and ink drawings.

The baroque exuberance of form which characterises the work of Ayrton; the tortuous fancy of Leslie Hurry and Robin Ironside; the more philosophic formulæ of Craxton and Collins, all carry on the major landscape tradition as it had been preserved by Paul Nash, and reinvigorated by Graham Sutherland. The difficulty of finding an adequate human notation has been a more perplexing task. Here the main influence perhaps has been Henry Moore. The sculptural conception of human form has a long history. Some of the later drawings of Poussin might have been drawn today, and throughout the inter-war period great advances were made by Wyndham Lewis, by William Roberts, and by Mark Gertler, but it was left to a sculptor finally to canalise the monumental aspects of the human body into a vocabulary of easily understandable artistic expression. If face to face with the problem of expressing humanity, however, the personal idiosyncrasies of the individual artist have fuller play. Ayrton is more profoundly influenced by the Northern Renaissance, Minton by a pictorial conception of the nostalgia of the Keatsian hero, whilst Vaughan is more genuinely humanistic in his preoccupation with direct social significances. Many of the older artists have evaded the problem entirely, and both Piper and Sutherland have not madeany real contribution. A more cogent influence has come from the non-English school, from the more painterly work of Jankel Adler, Robert Colquhoun and Robert Macbryde.

Most of the painters of promise in Britain today are young; it is a long time since there has been so much vitality of a non-derivative sort shown by men of thirty and under. The emergence of a coherent tradition, and the formulation of an iconography of force and simplicity may bring European painting to a last resting-place in the British Isles.

FIVE POEMS FROM IRELAND

chosen by

Robert Greacen

*

Valentin Iremonger

POEM

I bring you laughs and keep the tears myself
As I walk to you across the night
Who are the rich orchard of my delight
My wand of happiness, my wishing well

And all the pears of your aloofness fall
To gabble in these hot gardens like bursting children
Who glimpsed the daring of the witch's cauldron
And to their own burning gave no thought at all.

Love, I have wandered like a blinded Jew
And now, over the night, my promised land,
You wait for me, kiss in hand,
As lithely I step the remaining miles to you

Who can pin the winds like any insolent Spaniard
Or pierce the tide's malignant eye
With the needle of your happiness and joy.
So while tonight you are the fine vanguard

To cut the yellow harvest of my years
That flowers in the valley
Of my stony agony
I bring you laughs; I store away the tears.

Roy McFadden

FALL

Autumn, loose in the deep countryside,
Stay the stricken leaf's downfall, brown fall
That quickens grief for and a headlong pride
In all who died against the tyrants' wall,
Who fell because they served another world.
(Severe furled leaf, what master do you serve?
What hurricane of purpose caught and hurled
You forward in the pattern, crease on curve?)
We who in autumn pine for permanence
Among the raining leaves and running cloud,
Remembering the ringing utterance
Of bright belief transcending the mute crowd,
Await the word. The grey-eyed girl who smiles
In memory, polite acquaintances
And lifelong friends, seem only various styles
Without a meaning, lacking emphasis
Or the running rhyme that binds a world,
Without the word. Pale grey-eyed smiling girl
Moving among slow thought, have you the furled
Leaf's meaning in your love: the secret curl
Of silence, knot of knowledge binding all?
Then loose your love like hair in a dark tide
Of meaning for the brown leaf's fall, downfall,
The crumbling contours of this countryside.

Pearse Hutchinson

UPON THE SILENT SHORE

This evening of summer played masochistic truant
from the decreed pampering weather
of the seasons' kindergarten;
made even less buoyant my steps over a strand
sullen like a boy in detention,
barred of the tide, its boxing-the-fox, poach-in-the-stream
companion.

The fawn sand was a frown to see; like rope to the feel
of the feet; under the wall, strewn
dankly, the heaps of seaweed lankly
recalled the swill of rhubarb; sharp, then, as a rap
on the blackboard, pedagogue memory
drew my attention back to the date of a skirmish of infancy.

Launched by lemonade, father-led, shorts tucked hip-
high,
slow, from pools to the deep, I tip-toed;
shy of crabs, wicked shells, and pointed
pebbles—till, There! was the blue, blustering visor and
voice.
I broke from the kind, guiding hand,
scampering back to the kiss, the pail and the spade, and
more lemonade.

Sam Harrison

THE DANCERS

This is the Grand Pavilion
  where once the wanton music played,
hearty and heartless, for the sprightly dancers
under the dangling chandeliers' long icicles
    in that lost era of parade,
      complacency and bicycles,
which flourished twenty years, or so, before
my days began. Here's where they took the floor
    for polka, waltz-cotillion,
    schottische, valeta, lancers.

    Time, who can deftly alter
  summer to winter, noon to night,
with practised sleight of hand has cracked and crumbled
mirror and cornice, put his finishing touches
    on every reveller—made white
    the blackest of moustaches
and brought to grief each padded pompadour.
High-stepping masher, saucy paramour,
    caught in the self-same halter,
    by him, at last, are humbled.

    And yet the great magician
  has failed somehow, for all his pains,
tricks of the trade and hocus-pocus fingers,
to fool completely—in this faded splendour
    a subtler charm than his remains,
    compels us to surrender
our feelings to the past, almost as though
the dancers here, one night, were set aglow
    by some supreme emotion
    so strong that it still lingers.

Robert Greacen

FEAR VAMPS US ON

Fear gnaws the rope of afternoon,
Eats through its fibres one by one
And the startling nearness of June
Lifts the catch of the mental gun

That lies in wait for the mind's dark sequence.
The eyes in the mirror blink and stare;
A subtle eyelid arches in defence,
So that the idle rhododendrons flare.

Fear vamps us on across the hours
Through these cool evenings stretched as dreams,
Bathed in sweet-pulsing April showers
That come in silver-lightning streams.

Fear like a hollow corpse that putrifies
Spreads a cold stench from the curved nostril:
Fear puts death's sallow glaze on eyes
That survey ceaselessly, that look to kill.

Thus we are harried by despair,
Fear's passive moll: the saffron grin
Is everywhere unchallenged: the bare
Corroded teeth grimace in histrionic sin.

Fred Marnau

SOME NOTES AFTER
RE-READING FINNEGANS WAKE

*H*ave *you evew thought, wepowtew, that sheew gweatness was his twadgedy?* asks Sylvia Silence, the girl detective.

This is a Swiftian mirror of distortion, showing us how we really are, what asses: we cannot even talk. James Joyce is not as unintelligible as some prefer to think.

The God, however, must be sacrificed, so that everything can run smoothly and without any asocial interference. The girl detective speaks for every practical citizen when she regrets that He must *nevewtheless accowding to my considewed attitudes fow this act . . . pay the full penalty, pending puwsuance, as pew Subsec. 32, section 11, of the C.L.A. act 1885, anything in this to the contwawy notwithstanding.*

The harsher judgment is not for our well-bred ears. It is delivered through the keyhole by man's paid deliverer of insults, the reporter-informer. We shall never know whether it reached His ear, who *anarchistically respectful of the liberties of the noninvasive individual, did not respond a solitary wedgeword,* though, of course, it would have been easy for Him to reach with His hand beyond the limitations set by men and call His thunder, but He still hoped that the slanderer through the keyhole might be reformed by the peaceful means of educational and religious guidance of the *rowmish devowtion known as the howly rowsary,* the sound of which one could hear all the time from the near-by Dominican mission, while the accusing filth was shot at Him by the delegate from the new world: *Firstnighter . . . Yass We've Had His Badannas . . . Beat My Price . . . Tight before Teatime . . . Artist . . . Unworthy of the Homely Protestant Religion . . . Loose Luther . . . Go to Hellena or Come to Connies . . . Piobald Puffpuff His Bride . . .*

Barebarean . . . Peculiar Person . . . Flunkey Beadle Vamps the
Tune Letting on He's Loney . . . Easyathic Phallusaphist . . . In
Custody of the Polis . . . deposed . . . etc.

Why should it bother us, this obscure allegory of what?
This fermenting dungheap which is claimed to hold a letter,
a message, allegedly written by the low son of Him, H. C.
Earwicker? Why should we have been aware of it, and
troubled by its presence, ever since it was completed before
the war, in 1939? If a message was to be delivered to mankind, why not in plain language, so that everybody would
understand it? For was it not a most devilish and perverted
thing to do, to hide such a message, *if* there was one, behind
a forest of dark words, behind deliberately created obstacles
in the way of understanding by those who spent much time
and money on their education, and, further, to repulse the
innocent with foul language and litanies of insults? Why
reduce the majesty of God to the vile and suffering huge
body of an Irish innkeeper and God's succession to his sons
and daughters?

One might suggest that a few weeks after the completion
of this work the desired plain language had been uttered by
guns and call-up papers for six years without the slightest
effect, except to dull man further to the spectacle of sorrow.
The language of *Finnegans Wake* does at least provoke pro-
tests, contempt and bewilderment, as the fiercest critics, if
there be such 'fierce' critics, will admit. It may further be
said, that education is no key to the understanding of spiritual
matters; that the innocent are not repulsed by insult, they
cannot be touched by it and are aloof like Christ in the
house of Caiaphas and like Earwicker behind the keyhole;
that the majesty of God, descending into history, does take
part in our guilt and glory.

The darkness of *Finnegans Wake* is essential to it, and
therefore necessary and deliberate. We need not enter its
darkness, nor descend its comic steps into hell, but history
will prove to us that we cannot escape it in life. The promise
of *Finnegans Wake* is the promise of the possible exemption
from the compulsion of history; that by seeing it as a whole
we might escape the traps and remain untouched by its fires
until the final resurrection through the word comes.

So sit down by the waters of Babylon and laugh.

This strange book will not for ever remain closed to the superficial understanding. It is too objectionable and too inviting. Long passages have already become quite familiar, among them the famous description of Anna Livia Plurabelle. The poetry of it forces its way through the mist and overgrowth. In addition, learning, sacred and profane, and imagination will in time unriddle the outward locks. But this will only be a surface success. No amount of purely intellectual understanding will bring us the ultimate gift. This is what is so wonderful about *Finnegans Wake*, that you must be able to take part in the dream being dreamed, you must admit your forgotten childhood, your buried nights, your secret wisdom of both lands. *Finnegans Wake* urges your soul to be ready.

The explorer will return from its forests and wastes with many jokes and curious revelations, he will know all the measurements but, utterly unaware of the secret, he will miss the essential being of what he explored. Thus the deciphering of the text is a much overrated and superficial difficulty which research will overcome in time.

Finnegans Wake is first of all a religious book of the greatest importance to our age, since it proclaims the ever returning Christ. It seems odd to us because it *is* odd for this book to appear at just the appropriate moment; we are always puzzled by simple occurrences. The spectre of *Finnegans Wake* and the split atom belong to the same order of things. From a literary point of view *Finnegans Wake* is no more odd than that dozen books of which at least two in one volume are in every household.

Prejudice, laziness and fear can keep us from a true understanding of its dream-vision. The fear is justified, but relieved by Joyce's tremendous humour. The face of the sacrificed God is never shown to us unless it be blended with that of the eternal clown.

When history crosses the path of paradise, tragedy is born. Joyce seems to have reversed the position. He reduced history to successive explosions of comic events which overflood the paradisaical condition, fundamentally tragic, a loneliness shared with no one. Only slowly history, the clown, is absorbed again. We need not desire the synthesis of the tragic and comic through force of argument as Shem and Shaun do. For the eternal mother-river does not heed our achievement when she takes us back to our cold mad father, the ocean.

Indeed, our own time does not stand in the sign of unity but of dissolution. We move away from the failure of the baroque by being redeemed from the necessity to seek a synthesis. We may watch how the tensions and opposites weave their pattern on the loom of history, and wait until everything works out itself, wait and pray for the state of grace. The heroic deed is the unquestioning affirmation of life. This affirmation we are invited to share with James Joyce as all forms dissolve.

History broadens, its actions and gestures loosen, become uncontrollable, full of bloodshed and decay. The tendency of life is towards dust, not towards the dust of the grave, not towards the grave as the perfect enclosure of alchemical transition from which the angel is to rise. Nothing prepares for preservation. We see how futile the most terror-driven attempts towards political and civilisatory stabilisation are— for the blood is waiting to be spilt.

We are already carried by the flood together with all the other rubbish: *Godforsaken scapulars . . . cutthroat ties . . . quashed quotatoes . . . crocodile tears . . . presents from pickpockets . . . relaxable handgrips . . . fresh horrors from Hades . . . glass eyes for an eye . . . ahs ohs ous sis jas jos gias neys thaws sos yeses and yeses and tyses . . .*

The river, our virginal mother, obscures her husband, she covers the desecrated dismembered limbs of the earth, her broad delta devours greedily the last of him, going home, taking home our failings.

Behind her, where she began, her young lovely self is raining again from the little cloud; the naked nymph, untouched as yet by the comic, vile, brutal, absurd, life-giving thundering intercourse with history.

Terrible is the endless; how long, and to what purpose must we live for ever?

The cycle of the ages begins anew: loredom, foredom,

whoredom, and boredom. Foredom follows loredom, which is to come; whoredom was, boredom is now. That is history. But ever-present are man's two fundamental conditions: the ecstasy of the body, when he struggles with the beast; the mystery of the soul, when he labours to receive the Holy Ghost.

Our fires burn lowest now. But since we are utterly forsaken we are nearer to paradise than the preceding age, nearer, that is, to where we come from, where death and dream, life and poetry come from.

We were not a great success, and we are hurrying now to get it over with. We leave behind the cities and the laws, the statues and the triumphs, the Church and the hopes, the machines and the little chairs flying in the air.

The apple that hung on that tree in paradise has been exploded. We amuse ourselves in the dark with very quick things, shadow-playing, and lie immensely bored at the gates of heaven.

Shem and Shaun, the tree and the stone, the sons of HCE and ALP. That is us. The flocks, one on each side of the river, forever arguing the point until fog and night fall, and the washerwomen come and pick the rags of us up, and we know no longer that we missed the point.

Shem, the penman and Shaun, the postman; the one pens the message and the other delivers it. They are as long as life lasts, opposites, each on his side, the river between them. Throughout *Finnegans Wake* they represent the dualism of life in all its aspects, changing as history changes. They never meet until their common mother, regardless of their differences, takes them along into the dark night of transfiguration from whence they will rise again, twins again, duelling again in order to repeat the antagonism, the two-railed way of life.

They are not wholesome, these sons. Neither of them. They are but halves of their father. Shaun wishes to be the expanding side of him, the practical man of the world, the cheery chap, the empire-builder, the reassurer, the professor who knows all the answers; his books are best-sellers, he polices the world, and, incidentally, steals the messages from his brother. He explains it but fails to receive it. He is expansionistic, domineering, successful, and represents the cash-space outlook.

Shem is of very low character, unwashed, a loose fellow, asocial and introvert, constantly appealing for help from his brother. Historically he represents at times the mystical Celtic Church against the worldly Romish power of the jewel-studded staff of pope Adrian-Shaun. The reconciliation fails owing to the narrowest of waters dividing the two, a *most unconsciously boggylooking stream*, and owing to Shem-Gripes' whining but firm refusal to submit.

The drift widens, night falls, they lie all in pieces, each on his side; the old pagan women come and pick them up.

Shem is the poet, robbed of the message by his man-of-the-world brother who will never admit that he, too, is in need of his brother, but sells the message as his own discovery.

Shem represents essentially the dime-time aspect. He is his mother's darling, perpetually exiled and of tired eyes, *acheseyeld* like Joyce himself. Shem has as much of their common father as Shaun, though in accordance with his disposition he possesses all those qualities of him which are in opposition to those Shaun represents.

The more learned their quarrel becomes, the sillier sounds the argument to the eternal ears, the stupider, when they miss the call of nature, *Nuvoletta in her lightdress, spunn of sisteen shimmers, . . . looking down on them, leaning over the bannistars and listening all she childishly could.*

But, *The Mookse had a sound eyes right but he could not all hear. The Gripes had light ears left yet he could but ill see.*

Night falls with dark tears. A woman, *with chills at her feet,* gathers up *his hoariness the Mookse*; and there comes a woman, *comely, spite the cold in her head* and plucks down the Gripes. *And so the poor Gripes got wrong; for that is always how a Gripes is, always was and always will be. And it was never so thoughtful of either of them. And there was left now an only elmtree and but a stone. Polled with pietrous, Sierre but saule. O! Yes! And Nuvoletta, a lass.*

Shaun, desiring to take over the heritage of the father and to represent the message of the Holy Ghost, fails in both; Shem who has the message, is robbed of it. But he could not have delivered it to the people either, for different reasons from those of Shaun, who fails because he had only the wording, he could not steal the essence of the message. Shem fails naturally as the heir of his father; he received the Holy Ghost but was unable to save the race. They are sons, not fathers; their mother will soon take them away.

Finnegans Wake is a work of an ending age, of a final stage in human development. Tragedy and comedy intermingle again, without loosing their polarity and tensions. They produce a thunder which is part of the trumpeting noise to re-awaken the word. The language, too, widens like a delta, it overflows the banks and regulations and carries with it the fragments of numberless languages, past and present. It carries all their fables, legends, rhythms, slogans, nightmares and myths with its flood of anonymity. As if for the building of a new cathedral, Joyce assembled all these nameless forces through one unique creative act. He lifted, with more power than Michelangelo, all the great forgotten things like a tremendous monstrance and showed us, blessing and affirming, the golden mud of life, surrounded by the cycles of history, transfigured by the word.

Having seen the truth, grasped reality at last, the race has fulfilled the object of life. We may go home now. The ride and the hunt, the rule and the loving, the dream and the prayer are over. A holy madness moves into the mind, the body grows tired and bored. Our mother is due to end the tragi-comic tale of earth and water, innocence and experience, fall and resurrection.

We must not grudge the river sentimental recollections, our mother is old now. She knows us well; she is quite hard on us too, for she does not care to make us appear better than we are.

The language becomes quite orderly, this is an intimate dream-talk, we are not really meant to hear it; it is a tale whispered over our cradle-grave:

If I lose my breath for a minute or two don't speak, remember. Once it happened, so it may again. Why I'm all these years within years in soffran, allbeleaved. To hide away the tear, the parted. It's thinking of all. The brave that gave their. The fair that wore. All them that's gunne. I'll begin again in a jiffey.

The nymph, Nuvoletta, the little cloud, the fine rain that was in the beginning has become the grey broad suburban mother of the people. The ocean will transform her, she will be the young rain again, there will be Finn again. Already she is herself the little cloud far far back where she began. So let there be rain!

For she'll be sweet for you as I was sweet when I came down out of me mother. My great blue bedroom, the air so quiet, scarce a cloud. In peace and silence. I could have stayed up there for always only. Only, we cannot help taking part in life and history. *It's something fails us. First we feel. Then we fall.* Though we may loath it. *And I am lothing their warm little tricks. And lothing their mean cosy turns. And all the greedy gushes out through their small souls. And all the lazy leaks down over their brash bodies. How small it's all! And me letting on to meself always. And lilting all the time. I thought you were all glittering with the noblest of carriage. You're only a bumpkin. I thought you are the great in all things, in guilt and in glory. You're but puny. Home! My people were not their sort out beyond there as far as I can. For all the bold and bad and bleary they are blamed, the seahags. No! Nor for all our wild dances in all their wild din. I can see meself among them, allaniuvia pulchrabelled . . . I'll slip away before they're up. They'll never see. Nor know. Nor miss me. And it's old and old it's sad and old it's sad and weary I go back to you, my cold father, my cold mad father, my cold mad feary father, till the near sight of the mere size of him, the moyles and moyles of it, moananoaning, makes me seasilt, saltsick and I rush, my only, into your arms . . .*

This is how we die. Especially in our late centuries. The deaths and tears which we had not witnessed are quickening and broadening these lines, the mightiest our age has known. There is nothing so heavy with suffering and compassion and infinite beauty as the last pages of *Finnegans Wake*.

Soon the ages will begin again. Vico's vicious circle, theocratic, aristocratic, democratic, and chaotic. As the river runs past Eve and Adam's, the father-creator and our allsuffering mother, HCE and ALP, will transform the inspiration into the actions of life again.

Paul Potts

ABOUT WALT WHITMAN

EVERYTHING Walt Whitman wrote may not have been a work of art, but it was all, every huge untidy line of it, the work of an artist. He was the John the Baptist of a Christ, who has not yet arrived, but the water he used has flowed this far and still nourishes the longing for that Christ inside the human mind, as surely as the Atlantic is yet turning into surf, against Paumanok's shore. 'The Leaves of Grass' are like some enormous womb inside of which whole families of great and elegant desires await some fathering Holy Ghost. Real human greatness in a working-class person causes more trouble than a railway strike led by socialists. On his appearance, the middle brows form themselves into committees. Remember D. H. Lawrence and in an earlier time, William Blake. None of them could cope with Walt Whitman but few were able to ignore him. As the earth compels, so too real greatness is a target for viciousness, especially when it be unprotected by class or academic distinctions. Walt Whitman wasn't just another great writer. He was indeed something even more unique than that, if perhaps, in some ways, he was less. He wasn't a great man in the accepted sense of the word at all, he was a very ordinary man who possessed outstanding greatness. There have been many others, but one doesn't usually hear of them, except by the aid of some tragic accident as was the case with Bartolomeo Vanzetti. Of Whitman, David Gascoyne has written, 'he was congenitively incapable of despising anything on earth, this great humility has nothing to do with the morality of slaves, it is the mark of a really strong man and of an aristocrat'. It is a mistake to think of Whitman as a poet of the people in the great way that Burns and Mayakovsky and Lorca were. The whole style and form of his verse, if nothing else, would have prevented this. He was that rarer thing, a poet who could find no beauty where equality was missing and no freedom where ugliness remained.

One can no more think about Walt Whitman without speaking of America, than one could meditate on God without being conscious of Heaven. There is still a legend back in those states, that Lafayette, when he returned in triumph to the republic, which fifty years before he had assisted in establishing, picked up a small child, on the Brooklyn waterfront, and holding him up to the cheering crowds said in English, 'you should really be cheering this child you know, for here is the future of America', and the name of that child, was Walt Whitman. For what François Villon was to France and Dante to Italy, what Shakespeare was to England, what they were to the Renaissance and to the Middle Ages, Walt Whitman was to America and to that world in the beginning of which they were three words, Liberty, Equality and Fraternity. Yet he would have fully understood what the Negro poet Langston Hughes meant when he wrote,

'Let America be America again,
America never was America to me'.

Yet it was here in England and up in Canada that *The Leaves of Grass* were most appreciated on their first appearance. The Americans considered Whitman, almost European in his easy-going all embracing humanism. 'Not till the sun excludes you will I exclude you.' In this he was indeed to forestall Dostoevsky. His emphasis from the beginning was on equality and fraternity, as opposed to the classic American stressing of liberty. He believed that the only hope for beauty was to make everything beautiful. That the only chance liberty had of surviving was for all men to make themselves free. Unless the world is beautiful, a village will soon become ugly. Yet to the rest of the world he has always seemed more American than the stars and stripes themselves, the origin of which were, in fact, a private English gentleman's family coat-of-arms.

It should never be forgotten that in a certain very real sense England was a new country while Shakespeare was alive. This is even truer of Homer's Greece and Dante's

Italy. Yet during the great hey-day of American letters, throughout those glorious decades which have come to be known as the flowering of New England, when Boston, with Cambridge and Concord considered as daughter-republics, was in Spengler's opinion a culture city of a homogeneous commonwealth, as Florence, Bruges, and Weimar had been in other ages, the two really important American writers Herman Melville and Walt Whitman were almost, if not quite, ignored. Yet the real preface to *The Leaves of Grass* was not written by Whitman in 1855, but by Thomas Jefferson in 1776. Walt Whitman, who with Melville must be considered, by any standard of criticism, whatever the premises on which it is built, and from whatever angle it starts, providing of course that they be adequately serious, a major force in the whole of American literature, and was the first of her writers to come from that country's real working class. Through Whitman the American idea accepts everything and hopes for the best, while today the texture of that same human expression is perhaps best caught in the atmosphere of rejection and expectance of the worst to be found in the work of Henry Miller.

Walt Whitman's attitude to people, and it is this attitude which is his all-important contribution to the human republic, transgresses all adjectives, even the one adjective—American—which appears to qualify his every statement, and has percolated into his relations with everyone. He was indeed a man of all mankind. He would not accept anything from anybody unless it was offered to everyone else on equal terms. He was very religious but not about God, about man. Everything he wrote he knew belonged to others, it was their hopes that had loosened his tongue. No writer in any literature has so identified himself with his readers. He believed that there would never be great poetry until there were great audiences. Nowhere, other than in *The Leaves of Grass*, will you find exposed in so beautiful a setting, those things which are the common denominator in all men's make-up. As there is no garden, no field or allotment in which grass cannot grow, so too those things of which Whitman sings and talks and sometimes shouts can be found in the most intricate mind as well as in the simplest heart. Rareness is not of necessity an essential ingredient of beauty. The eye of a toad is so much more beautiful than that of an eagle. The one artist in nineteenth-century Europe, whose work did have a real affinity to that of the ageing Walt Whitman was the young Dutch painter Vincent Van Gogh. These two with the Russian composer Mussorgsky formed a sort of trinity, which could have acted as the fountain head of a new culture made from those ideas which all men hold in common. A culture which could have been formed if men were to add steel and concrete to this vision.

You can't have a child without sex, any more than you can have an apple without any pips, and you think when I concede you this, that you have won your argument. But you will never turn that child into a real human being, unless that child be wanted, and is loved. The one crest, the one lineage, the one nationality, the only breeding and the sole family tree, that is of the slightest use to anybody, and to which everyone is entitled, and without which no one of us, should ever have been born, is that it is right and proper to have a child, by anyone whom you love and who loves you, whatever the differences of race, class, age or colour, and by nobody else at all. If this be folly, then on the throne of Heaven there reigns a fool. No Isabella of any Castille, was ever asked, by a Columbus, for a ship, as *The Leaves of Grass* have waited for that world, of which they are but the precursory peninsulas. They are the coast line of a world, towards which a new Santa Maria is being ferried, by the winds of hope through this fog of current failure. I have tried desperately to remain restrained in writing this essay, because in whatever room I have lived since I left my nursery *The Leaves of Grass* have also always been an inhabitant too. In these poems of his, you will see what one means, when one says, that the whole basis of Democracy's claim to man's attention, are the very ideas and beliefs which are crowded into these American poems which have long since found their way into the minds of a few people and on to the shelves of most libraries in every country in the world.

When as a child one sat on one's father's knee, all one saw was his face and his waistcoat. When standing, one seldom got much further than his knees, all that towered above was out of focus. Some things are too large to be seen in their entirety at a glance. How few are they, who have seen the whole of a whale. This has long since been Walt Whitman's fate. If, then, he is too big to get into the first part of a lifetime, how difficult it must be to get him into an essay. While the world is evil, goodness will always cause trouble. His name has been a battle-field for literary critics since Emerson hailed the first edition of *The Leaves of Grass*, a few weeks after its publication in 1855, by telling all the Americans to come home from Europe, 'as, unto us a man is born, unto us the word is given'. It is interesting to note, that although since the days of Benjamin Franklin and Joel Barlow, through Washington Irving, Hawthorne, Hemingway and Harte Crane down to the last Cunarder that docked in Cherbourg, a feature of the American literary scene has always been the number of ex-patriates living in Europe, that the one American writer whose work went furthest afield, never left the American continent, even for a pleasure cruise.

They can say what they like about Walt Whitman. But whosoever believes and has the courage and the sense to act upon that belief, that beauty is the private property of all men and not merely the privilege of the few, will love Walt Whitman and his ferry boats, his horse-drawn trams and his yawp, his litanies and his catalogues, his Pete Doyle and his Abraham Lincoln, his contradictions and his self-assertions, his huge hungry dreams and his few great lyrical poems that are equal to all, and are surpassed by none of the great poems of this language.

Walt Whitman is something new in the literary history of the world. Unlike almost any other great man, his life was the life of an ordinary person. He was never a success, he had more difficulty in getting an editor to accept a poem at fifty-five than Stephen Spender did when he was twenty-five. Unlike most people who possess it, Whitman's literary greatness never protected him from the rough and tumble of the ordinary life of a person of no position and small means. He had no Ayot St. Lawrence, no town house, no publisher was ever in a hurry to print him, no committees rushed to shower him with literary awards. He was always a target for the viciousness of the usual nonentities who form so large a fraction of any literary community. He was never popular with the public. Yet he did save a little money, about as much as a rank and file member of the N.U.R.

might save today. Tennyson wrote to him affectionately, and he thought the Poet Laureate to be the greatest poet of the age. While Oscar Wilde called on him in Mickle Street and found there, that 'state republican, where every man's a king', which he missed in Belgravia. And he was loved by most people who knew him.

Walt Whitman was the first to put the modern idea of human equality into literary form. He was more gentle, than nearly all gentlemen, yet he had more in common with all men, than a very normal average bank clerk has. This funny old eccentric had more courage than the worldly Mark Twain. This bachelor had more love for children than most fathers. This homo-sexual had more real affection for women than a Casanova. There in the words of Ezra Pound, perhaps the one truly great, among the many near-great men, of his nationality, who have followed Walt Whitman in his vocation, is a whole generation's attitude to him.

> I make a pact with you, Walt Whitman
> I have detested you, long enough
> I come to you as a grown child
> Who had had a pig-headed father
> I am old enough to make friends
> It was you who broke the new wood
> Now is a time for carving
> We have one sap and one root
> Let there be commerce between us.

Inside *The Leaves of Grass* there is material for building. Enough to stretch a world to hold a dream. Here among the wealth of this material Walt Whitman pondered, on love and living, on hatred of the sham. He would not sell one lath of this material, for some emparked lake dotted monarchy. Literature has indeed had many great men, but he was her only great child. Walt Whitman would not hurt a butterfly, but neither was he afraid of a bully.

146

Patricia Hutchins

ASPECTS OF
SCIENCE AND THE CINEMA

'... *science with all its consequences is not such a desperately serious affair and all things considered, it contributes less to the material well being than is generally assumed, while it contributes more than is generally assumed to purely ideal pleasures.*' Science, Art and Play, *from* Science and the Human Temperament, *by Erwin Schrodinger.*

BECAUSE there is no separateness, only the individual tasting of the stream of experience, drops scooped into the palm of one's hand, running so quickly through the fingers, we see reflected in the cinema as in so much of art and literature an attempt to summarise, to know all, be everywhere. The film thus becomes part of our concern with time, with number and the telescoping of space made possible by scientific development. Orlando cutting love-initials on the bark of trees in the forest of Arden, Joyce seeing in the blurred outlines of Switzerland and Paris memory-patterns of another place and period, Virginia Woolf listening to the typewriter chatter of young herons, watching a moth die—all creative work has been a protest, a greediness for further life.

Our appetite expresses itself in different ways, according to temperament, education, circumstance. Some take to sport or love-making, others to hobbies, cultural and scientific activity. The film has often been called a drug, a means of escape from reality. Yet who wants to be continually with the pots and pans, the basic conditions of existence? What matters is the material we bring back from the further countries of the imagination and how it is to be adapted into the system of 'every-day'; for each influence, however slight, has a bearing on our own future and that of society as a whole.

The scientific film can also be regarded as an excursion into other dimensions, worlds greater or smaller than our own. It provides a means of recording facts and exploring fresh possibilities, an opportunity for putting forward new developments and ideas. The work of the scientist, and his publicist, thus represents an optimistic attitude; while more and more ability of various kinds tends to use the screen as a means of expression, there remains a fairly good chance that something of our civilisation may survive.

Like the microphone, the cinema in this sense has no use for snob values. It breaks down the divisions between one section of research and its neighbour, fusing, intermingling many different subjects, and in the documentary, often serving to bring them back from the laboratory, the workshop or the office into direct relationship to ordinary life, shown in terms of men and women, familiar places and objects. Whereas the dignity and impersonalness of print had made it possible for the pedant to hide his limitations behind long words and difficult expositions, now we do not ask 'What is Browning's law?' so much as 'Why is it important to us?'

The recent catalogue of some six hundred 'Films of General and Scientific Interest available in Great Britain', ranges from a summary of how oil is produced, a demonstration for factory workers, an account of *William Harvey and the Circulation of the Blood* sponsored by the Society of Medicine, to a series on the care of children's eyes and teeth. In between are a diversity of other subjects—*Heredity in Man, Tomato Growing, Neuro-psychiatry*. This catalogue was compiled by the Scientific Film Association which aims at promoting 'the national and international production and use of the scientific film in order to achieve the widest understanding and appreciation of the part which science can play in the modern world'.

The cinema came into being as a divided personality, or shall we say a twin, being regarded as a means of diversion on the one hand and a method of research on the other. We know what big brother Box-office has become, but the serious child, the film in relation to humanity as a whole, has not yet reached full development. Given a fair chance this may eventually control the excesses of the entertainment side. In 1872 Muybridge had anticipated the use of slow motion in setting up twelve still cameras to illustrate his contention that a galloping horse lifts all four feet from the ground. Eventually one camera came to replace the dozen and it was soon realised that the cinema presented great possibilities of control, through the slowing down or acceleration of the time-factor. Here was a watcher of infinite patience and reliability, recording, for instance, the growth of a flower at regular intervals. When these single observations are run together through the projector, as the spokes of a revolving wheel appear as one, so the process appears to happen before our eyes.

Percy Smith was another pioneer. From the building of his first machine for filming plant life in 1910, to the famous *Secrets of Nature* series, he brought to the material which gradually became available as camera combined with the greater eye of the microscope, that selectiveness and sense of proportion which made these films generally popular. Other productions with the teaching of biology as their chief objective, such as *The Development of the Trout* supervised by Dr. Julian Huxley, and experiments in Dufaycolour, led on to Smith's last film, *The Life Cycle of the Pin Mould*. To quote the catalogue already mentioned, 'Beautifully photographed and well-planned, it shows a fungus as a living organism and not as a series of structures at discreet intervals of time'.

'It is with the complexities of the living processes, both in the study of plant life and the animal kingdoms, that the film really comes into its own as the recording medium *par excellence*', wrote J. D. Durden in an article on films and micro-biology in *Documentary News Letter* of January-February 1937. Early on, valuable work concerning the growth of cancer cells had been carried out by the late Dr. Canti, using the time-lapse technique, now employed in many different ways.

The present writer has been fortunate in seeing a remarkable series of films, produced by Dr. Commondon and M. de Fronbrune of the Department of Cinemicrophotography of the Institut Pasteur over the past decade or so. These provide observations of little understood phenomena which could not be studied so well by any other method. One of these films deals with the reactions of the nucleus during cell division; another the activities of the white corpuscles in the blood, while the feeding powers of the single cell organism Amoeba and the life of a carnivorous, soil growing fungus provide other themes. To undertake these and similar investigations, to manipulate, give food or dissect under the microscope, it has been necessary to make tiny instruments by means of the 'micro-forge', a process also demonstrated on the screen.

As workmanlike in approach, the films of Jean Painlevé deal chiefly with submarine life. From the early *Sea-Horses* to the recently completed *Assassins d'Eaux Douces*, with a background of weird underwater forests and caves, they convey something more than zoological curiosities, being presented with such adroitness and humour that at moments these productions stand as an example of science become art.

At the other extreme, often suggesting a visual parallel between micro- and macrocosm, are those films being made in various countries from the U.S.A. to China, to record and analyse different aspects of astronomy. The phases of an eclipse, with its momentary effect on plants and animals, or great slowly rising flames upon the sun's surface, these seem all the more striking when presented silently. On the other hand one remembers how well current theories were summarised in the documentary *Boundless Universe* made by U.F.A., in which diagrams and models were often related most effectively to a realistic setting.

Whereas the contrast of black and white with its intermediate gradations of tone, however badly handled, left the eyes indifferent, in peace, the use of colour has, on the whole, placed a filter of disconcerting unreality between the viewer and the screen world. As with the puppet and cartoon film, in the scientific and instructional field, the range of contrasts is often more under control and where the subject matter is unusual, one accepts the deliberately used distortion. Medical films in particular will continue to benefit by the development of good 16 mm. in colour, with its stereoscopic possibilities.

It was not until 1936 that any serious attempt was made to

sort out and list the different categories into which medical films had shaped themselves, Many which had been made by surgeon or physician for demonstration purposes or to record a technique, suffered from poor photography and presentation. The present tendency is to study the means more closely or to collaborate with the professional film-maker, while interesting experiments are being carried out by Units set up in a number of the medical schools and the universities. Outstanding among recent developments are a series of eleven films, sponsored by I.C.I., on anæsthetic techniques, designed specially for students.

As emphasis shifts from cure to prevention, there will surely be an increasing number of films dealing with public health and hygiene. *Defeat Diphtheria, Blood Transfusion, Birthday,* a study of infant mortality rates, are productions which have already reached immense audiences outside the entertainment cinemas. Documentary producers, with their strong social awareness, continue to press for a clearly defined policy. Behind them stand the achievements of the thirties, and the films of war-time effort have given place to *The Way We Live* dealing with the planning of Plymouth and a further film study of conditions and their remedy has been sponsored by Manchester City Council. This then is part of the 'art of presenting science,' and as Grierson has put it, 'Documentary is at once a critique of propaganda and a practice of it.'

Much of the past has not yet slipped so far away behind us that a record might no longer be made of certain phases. The anthropologist can use the camera in the study of man against his natural background. Social historian and folk-lore collector can still save valuable data in those countries where types of houses, implements, tradition and modes of speech and music, have not yet disappeared into the mixer of present-day influences. Soon it may be too late and the many ingredients will have set in a different composition, like the concrete pavements that seal over the paths and lanes of what was once countryside now become town.

The film often seems to reconcile the opposites of extreme specialisation and the way in which all branches of knowledge are part of a particular tree, that of human consciousness as a whole. It is both impersonal in its command of distance and diversities of peoples, the juxtaposition of objects and physical conditions. Forming a kind of reservoir of association it is like a vast mind contained by the envelope, the shell if you like, of the 'I'. Watching the development of the newt in an instructional film or following the success or disaster of a personal story, we tend to undergo a process of identification—a relationship to this many-runged ladder of evolution, or a suffering and joy undertaken by proxy, for which we feel in some way responsible.

In an interesting but somewhat heterogeneous collection of theories and questionnaires, J. P. Meyer's *Sociology of Film* represents an admittedly subjective approach. Certainly the net is spread very wide and all sorts of fish jump about in it—the influence of Levy Bruhl's studies of the primitive mind, Malinowski's interpretation of myth, Plato, Aristotle, Elizabethan drama, and the naïve opinions of the school-girl and the typist. 'What is really important to the sociologist,' he states, 'is the discovery and isolation of the implicit attitudes of a motion picture, the general assumptions on which are based the conduct of the characters and the treatment of situations of the plot.' The film-maker himself can be of great value when he is able to define both his own approach and the influences at work within (during production) and without a film—as seen by the audience.

During the war, films were used with regard to questions of industrial psychology and personnel selection. The rehabilitation of war neurosis has been recorded and remarkable data presented to the specialist. Now the Tavistock Institute of Human Relations brings together Army and civil psychiatrists to co-operate with the film-makers. Not only will the family, in relation to the community, the outlook of political and cultural groups be investigated but long-term research is planned to show more precisely how the cinema influences old values and introduces new ones.

The effect of background music will also be considered. In passing, it is interesting to note what one might call the 'neurotic theme' now accompanying sections of certain entertainment films. Very effective in such instances as *Lost Weekend*, it has since become a *cliché*, there being nothing so copy-cat as the mediocre producer. Yet this and other

YOUNG SEA-HORSE BEFORE ASSUMING VERTICAL POSITION
'Sea-horses' by Jean Painlevé

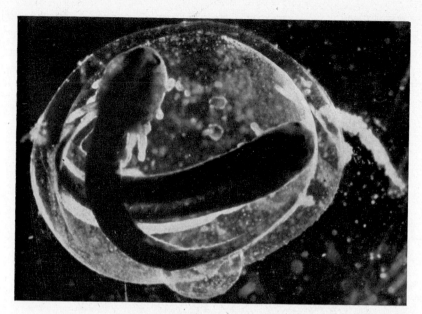

THE FORMATION OF TWINS
Film by U.F.A.

BOUNDLESS UNIVERSE
Film by U.F.A.

devices do prepare the way for the acceptance of more carefully considered themes touching on abnormal states of mind. The cinema's power to draw us into the issues involved can thus be directed towards the means of coping with the entanglement of personal relationships, the ethical and often religious difficulties which may arise.

One no longer asks the boy or girl what books they read, so much as 'What films have you seen lately and what are your favourite stars and stories?' From the reply we learn something about the child and much about the cinema. Not only the emotional and intellectual development of children is being annotated by both amateur and professional film-maker, a study made of reaction to home and school conditions, the interplay of community life, but some good films have dealt with juvenile delinquency and other social problems.

As part of an experimental scheme to use films in the schools which is likely to have far-reaching effects on education as a whole, the Visual Unit may prove as revolutionary as Caxton's press. Planned by the Ministry of Education with the advice of experts on particular subjects and teachers themselves, these films with their appendages of strip-film, special handbook of further information and wall-charts, aim at 'covering in a broad manner a rounded area of knowledge'. Their subject matter overflows the narrow channels of the ordinary curriculum and carries many different aspects on the same stream of sustained interest. Here are everyday, out-of-classroom things given a new and more dramatic significance, linked to the life of the countryside or town, forming part of the pupil's own.

This may suggest that lecturer or teacher can allow the film to take his place, whereas these new techniques demand a great deal of attention and enthusiasm. Besides material difficulties to be overcome, such as the nation-wide provision of sound film apparatus and sufficient films to serve them, the training of teachers and lecturers to their full use, there is also a forest of prejudice to be cleared and replanted. Yet the educationalist and the historian of the future may find that the introduction of visual aids for both children and older groups will have served to break up the present system, still faced by the blackboard and the dry paged text book in many instances, the removed-from-life atmosphere of the examination hall. Underlying this work will be the principle of adjustment, the relationship of individual effort to that of the community, the full use of the personality.

The Scientific Film Society movement has already brought many films of interest before a growing and varied membership. Developed from the work of the Association of Scientific Workers, there first came the London Scientific Film Society and now some dozen groups have been established in England and Wales. Shows for children have also been given in London and the provinces. It may be possible in future to see many more of the scientific and documentary films made abroad. Plans are being formulated for the expansion of the very successful *Congrès du Film Scientifique et Technique* held in Paris during the past ten years, into a world gathering there of all those interested in the serious cinema.

It seems as if the creative mind has often presaged the forms later established as fact by that doubter, the Thomas we call scientist. Many of the living patterns shown by the combination of microscope and ciné-camera seem surrealist. Shelley in *The Cloud* certainly realised the experience of flying 'to pass over the rills and the crags and the hills. Over the lakes and the plains'. Only in a very few instances has talent near to genius yet found in the cinema a means of merging art and science into one. Later the distinction may almost cease to exist; writers and psychologists now share the same territory; our physicists become philosophers.

THREE DIRECTIONS IN FRENCH WRITING

edited and introduced by

Derek Stanford

★

INTRODUCTION

MAN is a vassal of the external world, a creature
of dependence, a behaviouristic puppet: such
has been the import of many current theories
concerned with interpreting human life. Op-
posed to this depreciation of freedom and personal identity,
three tendencies in the literature of France are clearly manifest today; namely, Surrealism, Existentialism, and the great
upsurge of lyricism in prose and verse.

Before considering the contemporary position, a word on
the past is perhaps required; a sketch of the former attitude
from which the present now powerfully reacts.

Long before the description of man by Marx, Freud, and
Watson as a wire-pulled doll, subject to unconscious or
inanimate forces, had become an influential notion, this
same deterministic hypothesis had established itself in
French art and thought. In his brilliant *History of English
Literature* the critic Taine explained the individual under
three somewhat hard-and-fast headings: 'race, epoch, and
surroundings'. According to this analysis, man was the sum
of component parts, the product of an addition of facts, a
biped machine of bones and flesh. Out of theories such as
this, arose the novels of Realism: the great sociological
sequence of Zola—a more intellectual and logical Dickens.

The first European culture in the field to create a thorough-
going realistic art, it is natural that the pendulum-swing
from this position should first be observed in the literature
of France.

'Triumph over causality', significance of personal decision, and thirdly, a poetry of mind-over-matter: these are
three factors stressed by this new writing.

The first of these is the battle-cry of all Surrealistic work:
the frantic desire and determination to break the vicious
circle of ends-and-means in a world where both are singu-
larly corrupt. 'France is fallen, and you are defeated. Therefore your ideology is dead', so the invading Nazi reasoned,
respecting the links of cause-and-effect. Heir to a great
imaginative tradition, that might well adopt as its proud
motto the words of the German Schopenhauer 'The world is
my representation', the Surrealist turned away unimpressed.

'Let him despise all prohibitions', Bréton had written in
1929, 'and let him make use of that avenging weapon, the
idea, against the beastliness of all beings and all things, and
let him on the day when he is defeated . . . treat the firing
of the pathetic rifles as a volley of salute.'[1] Armed with such
early exhortations, believing the dream and the waking-day
are one, the Surrealist artist was unconcerned by the capture
of the mere outer husks of his world. Inside him he carried
his own sphere of freedom; infinite reserves of assertion and
escape. Reality assumed the colour of his wishes. He, not
external history or matter, was the true stage-manager of his
own life. One wave of his hand, and the scene was changed
according to the creative dictates of his choice. 'This summer', wrote Bréton in 1924, 'the roses are blue; the wood is
made of glass. The earth wrapped in its foliage makes as
little effect on me as a ghost.'[2] Of what use talking to such a
man—equipped with his self-expanding universe—of the
unanswerable logic of events! Freedom is something one
bears inside one, which outside tyranny cannot take away.
So Eluard—poet of the unfallen France—in a conquered
country was able to write

> 'And by the power of a word
> I recommence my life
> I am born to know you
> To name you
> Liberty.'[3]

[1,2] Translated by David Gascoyne.
[3] Translated by Roland Penrose and E. L. T. Mesens.

If Surrealism be described as an imaginative assertion of free-will, then Existentialism must appear as the ethical counterpart of this. 'I am what I imagine', the Surrealist maintains: 'I am what I decide', the Existentialist answers. The first sees man as the fruit of his own desire: the second views him as the child of his own decision. 'Man is nothing', writes Sartre, 'but what he makes of himself. This is the first principle of Existentialism. It is, too, what is called subject-ivism, and under this name is held against us. But what do we mean by that term but that man has a greater dignity than a stone or a table? For we mean in the first place, that man exists, that is to say that man is first of all a being who directs himself towards a future, and who is conscious of projecting himself into the future.'[4] This insistence on individual free-will has, in the past, gone hand-in-hand with given values, from the system of Aquinas to that of Kant. With these, Existentialism begs to differ. If man has the free-will to be his own maker, the values he observes will be likewise of his making. The only absolutes are our acts of decision.

The third bid for freedom in the literature of France is the tendency to lyricism; an imaginative spate of prose poems and verse. This former genre of composition—a stranger almost to English letters—has played an integral part in French writing; is accepted as a species in its own right. From the work of St. John Perse, Eluard and Cocteau, to that of Henri Michaux and René Char, the prose poem has flourished in modern French culture as the near - but not the poor-relation of verse. Many French poets have indeed employed both, including—to name but a few at random—Apollinaire, Cocteau, Eluard, Reverdy, Max Jacob, Bréton, and Tour du Pin. As corollary, perhaps, to this condition, one finds certain poets such as Aimé Césaire whose verse is a kind of chanted prose. The trafficking between these two media is heavy.

This lyrical uprising seems to have its source in this same wish to assert one's freedom and realise one's identity, in a world committed to oppose both of these, as the other two movements already mentioned. This world must be changed,

[4] Translated by Henry Parris.

wrote Rimbaud and Marx; and he who cannot transform it by action may overcome it in terms of song. Just such a kind of latter triumph was surely the singing of Orpheus. Eurydice still remained dead, it is true; but grief in the act of becoming music was sublimated and turned to account . . . grew to be a sort of harmonious pain.

Prisoners of a society which jails and persecutes our hopes, many French poets have chosen this way out—this total-fantasy-exploration art; escapism on a creative scale. This term, reserved as a rule for derogation, must be understood in another sense here. To raise the problems of existence on to the level of make-belief and song is not to avoid or ignore their nature, but merely to deal with them on a different plane. Once this act of levitation has been made, the burden will be shouldered in an individual fashion; the technique of wrestling with sorrow and chaos assuming with each poet a unique form.

So for St.-John Perse the task appears as that of constructing the universe anew; 'a kind of sublime state of civilisation', as Roger Caillois, has remarked, 'made with the essence of those known in history, but surpassing them in greatness and majesty'.[5] '*Eloges, Anabase,* and *Exil* are voyages', the critic Wallace Fowlie observes of this work, 'not literal in any geographical sense, but great caravan explorations of the soul, moments filled with the action of progress and conquests'. 'Each line', he continues, 'creates its own form, as if the voyage which is the quest for the reality of things—or what we might call the holiness of things—was a moving into the unknown and the untested.'

Another device for dealing with defeat, for making frustration eloquent, is that which Henri Michaux employs and which he describes as 'Exorcism', 'Into the very roots of suffering and obsession such exaltation', he writes, 'is introduced, such magnificent violence, united by the hammer-blows of words, that the malady, progressively dissolved, is replaced by an airy and demoniacal ball—a wonderful state to be in!'[6] In his work we find the rare example of stoicism grown lyrical; the will to endure has resulted in a song, in a chant of determined perseverance.

[5] Translated by Walford Morgan.
[6] Translated by James Kirkup

158

To write beyond the boundaries of good and evil is one of the canons of surrealist poetics: to write beyond hope and despair, however, is an even more arduous uphill task. 'This vertical and explosive ascension', writes Michaux, 'is one of the great moments of existence. It can hardly be sufficiently recommended to those who live, in spite of themselves, in unhappy dependency. But it is difficult to get the motor started; only an almost total despair will do it.'[7]

These are but two techniques for snaring freedom, for possessing one's identity in poetic form. Along with others, these poets understand that freedom is not a gift from the State, but rather a condition one creates for oneself; the reverse of the coin of responsibility. This is not to say that politics have no part to play in achieving freedom. As defence and guarantee of a generous social floor-space, of a wide arena of ample living, they have their own contribution to make. They provide the collectively suitable site. Upon this, however, we must each build our house, and attempt to rear the walls of individual freedom. Sometimes we must do this without their help; without their previous communal preparation. Such times, it seems, are with us now. We give thanks to the poets who have shown us the way.

[7] Translated by James Kirkup.

Henri Michaux

THE JETTY

AFTER living for over a month in Honfleur, I still had not seen the sea, for my doctor made me keep to my room.

But yesterday evening, weary of this isolation, I constructed, under the cover of fog, a jetty which reached to the sea.

Then, sitting right at the end with my legs dangling over the edge, I watched the deep-breathing sea beneath me.

A murmur came from my right. It came from an old man who was sitting like me with his legs dangling, and who was watching the sea. 'Now that I am old', he was saying, 'I am going to draw out everything I have put into it during all these years.' He began to haul in, making use of pulleys.

And he drew out an abundance of riches. He brought up, in full-dress uniform, sea-captains of a bygone age, nail-studded chests containing all sorts of precious things, and women richly dressed but wearing clothes such as they no longer wear. And he would look carefully and very hope-fully at each creature or object that he brought to the sur-face, then without a word, with hope dying in his eyes, he would shove it behind him. In this manner we filled the whole jetty. My memory is poor, so I cannot remember exactly all there was, but obviously he was not satisfied with it, there was something lacking in it all, something he had hoped to find but which had withered away.

So he began to throw everything back into the sea.

It was like a long ribbon which, as it fell, soaked you through and chilled you. He shoved off one last article and was carried away by it himself.

As for me, shivering with fever, how on earth I got back to my bed Heaven only knows.

('Mes Propriétés')   (*Translated by James Kirkup*)

MY STATUES

I HAVE my statues. The centuries have bequeathed them to me: the centuries of my waiting, the centuries of my discouragements, the centuries of my indefinitions, of my unquenchable hope have made them. And now they are there.

Like ancient debris they lie: I do not always know just what they are supposed to represent.

Their origin is unknown to me and is lost in the night of my living, where their shapes alone have been preserved in the inexorable sweeping-away.

But they are there and their marble hardens every year a little more. They are there, whitening the obscure background of forgotten masses.

('Epreuves, Exorcismes')   (*Translated by James Kirkup*)

MY ESTATES

ON my estates everything is flat, nothing moves; and if there is a shape here and there, where does the light come from? There is no shadow.

Occasionally, when I have time, I observe, holding my breath: on the watch: and if I see something emerging, I'm off like a shot and pounce on the place, but the head, —because it is most often a head—sinks back into the mud; I dig a hole, quickly, but there is only mud, or sand, sand . . .

There is no beautiful blue sky either. Although there seems to be nothing overhead, one has to walk with one's back bent as if one were in a low tunnel.

These estates are all I have; I have lived there since my childhood and I may say that few people possess more unprofitable ones.

Often I thought of laying it out in beautiful avenues, of making a great park . . .

Not that I care much for parks, but anyhow . . .

At other times—(it's a mania I have, an inexhaustible mania that flourishes in spite of all repulses), I see in the outer world or in an illustrated book an animal I like, a white tufted heron for example, and I say to myself: 'Now that would look well on my estates, and besides, that sort of thing might multiply', and I make lots of notes and look up information about everything concerning the animal's life. My documentation gradually assumes vast proportions. But whenever I try to transport the animal to my domains, it always has a few essential organs missing. I flounder. I sense already that nothing will come of it this time either; and as for multiplying, on my estates nothing ever multiplies, I know that only too well. I look after the new arrival's food, its appearance, plant trees for it, sow grass, but the nature of my estates is such, that if I turn my attention to something else, or if I am called away for one minute, when I come back there is nothing left, or only a thin layer of ash, which, at the very most, conceals one last sprig of rusty moss . . . at the very most.

But if I go on trying, it is not stupidity on my part.

It is because I am condemned to live on my estates and because I have to do something or other with them.

I shall soon be thirty years old, and I still have nothing; naturally I am beginning to feel rather fed-up.

I can manage to form an object, or a thing, or a fragment. Like a branch or a tooth, or a thousand branches and a thousand teeth. But where can I put them all? There are people who quite effortlessly produce ranges of mountains, multitudes, ensembles.

Not I. A thousand teeth, yes, a hundred thousand teeth, yes, and some days on my estate I have a hundred thousand lead-pencils, but what can you do in a field with a hundred thousand lead-pencils? They just don't fit in, unless you have a hundred thousand draughtsmen.

All right. But while I am working on a draughtsman (and as soon as I have one, I shall have a hundred thousand), lo and behold my hundred thousand lead-pencils have disappeared.

And if for the tooth I prepare a jaw, and an apparatus for digestion and excretion, as soon as the outer casing is completed, when I am just about to put in the pancreas and the liver (for I always work most methodically), the teeth have disappeared, and then the jaw as well, then the liver, and when I reach the anus, there is nothing left but the anus (disgusting), because if I have to retrace my steps by the colon, the small intestine, and the biliary vesicle and all the rest—well, no.

In front and behind everything is immediately eclipsed, it cannot stay still for one instant.

Now I can't just wave a wand and make complete animals; I proceed methodically, otherwise it is impossible.

And that is why my estates are absolutely devoid of anything, except for one being, or a series of beings; which only has the effect of emphasising the general poverty, and putting a monstrous and unbearable trade-mark on the prevailing desolation.

Then I suppress everything and there is nothing left but marshes, nothing else but marshes, which constitute my sole estate and which will drive me to despair.

And still I keep on trying, though I really don't know why.

But sometimes it all comes to life, things begin to stir. It can be seen, it is no idle fancy. I always *did* suspect that there was something there, and so now I feel full of enthusiasm. But along comes a woman from the outer world; and overwhelming me with pleasures, innumerable but so close together that they all last no longer than a second: and carrying me away in that same second, carrying me many, many times right round the world . . . (for my part, I never dared ask her to visit my territories in their present poverty-stricken state of quasi-inexistence). Well! on the other hand, quickly worn out by so many incomprehensible voyages which were no more than a breath of perfume, I run away from her, cursing women once again, and completely lost on this great planet, I weep for my estates, which are nothing, but which after all are familiar ground, and do not give me that feeling of *absurdity* that I find everywhere else.

I spend weeks, humiliated, alone, looking for my estates; at such moments people can call me whatever abusive names they please.

The only thing that keeps me going is the conviction that it is not possible for me not to find my land; and indeed, one day sooner or later, there it is in front of me again!

What joy to find oneself back again on one's own land! It really never looks quite like anything else. There may be a few changes—it seems to me to be sloping a little more, or more humid; but the texture of the earth, that is always the same.

Maybe it doesn't bring me abundant harvests. But all the same, this peculiar texture of the earth—it says something to me. However, if I go closer, it becomes part of the mass— a mass of little haloes.

Never mind, it is, quite definitely, my own land. I cannot explain it, but I could never mistake another for it. It would be as if I mistook someone else for myself, which is impossible.

On one side is my land and myself: the rest, on the other side, is unknown land.

There are some people who have magnificent estates, and I envy them. They see something that they like somewhere. Right, they say, I'm going to have that for my estate. No sooner said than done, and the thing is on their estate. How is this brought about? I don't know. From childhood onwards, practised in collecting, acquiring things, they have only to see a thing and they plant it immediately in their own grounds, and it all happens quite automatically.

One can't even call it greed. It is a sort of reflex action.

Many are hardly aware of it. They have magnificent estates that they keep up by the constant exercise of their intelligence and their extraordinary abilities, and they are quite unaware of what they are doing. But if you need a plant, however rare, or an old carriage such as was used by Joan V of Portugal, they go away for a moment and bring you back at once whatever you asked for.

Those who are good at psychology, and I don't mean the sort you find in books, will maybe have noticed that I have been telling lies. I said that my property is an estate. Well it was not always like that. The estate is on the contrary a very recent acquisition, though to me it seems so ancient, and even seems to span several existences.

I am trying to remember exactly what my estates were like before.

They were like whirlwinds; like vast pockets, like faintly-luminous purses, and made of an impalpable but very thick material.

Sometimes I have to meet a very old friend. The tone of the conversation soon becomes very painful. Then I rush off to my property. It is shaped like a cross. It is large and luminous. There is daylight in this illumination, and a compass-needle that shakes like water. And I am at ease there; this lasts for a few moments, then, for politeness' sake, I go back to the young lady and I smile. But this smile has such a peculiar quality . . . (possibly because it excommunicates her), that she goes out slamming the door.

That's the sort of thing that goes on between my friend and myself. It's a regular thing.

We would do better to separate once and for all. If I had large and prosperous estates obviously I would leave her. But with the present state of things, it is best to wait a little while longer.

But to get back to my property. I was talking about despair. No. Land, on the contrary, authorises every hope. One can build on land, and I shall build. Now I am sure of it. I am saved. I have a firm basis.

Before, as everything was in the void, without ceiling, without floor, naturally if I put a creature inside, I never saw it again. It would disappear. *Disappear by falling*. That is something I had never understood; and there was I thinking I had not constructed it correctly! I used to come back a few hours after having put the thing inside, and was always astonished to find it had disappeared. Now, that will happen no more. My land, it is true, is still marshy. But I shall drain it gradually, and when it is firm and hard, I will put a whole family of workmen on it.

It will feel good to walk on my land. Wait till you see the things I shall do with it! My family will be enormous. You will find all types in it. I still haven't shown it to you, but you will see it. And its evolutions will be the wonder of the world. For it will evolve with that avidity and that passion peculiar to people who have lived too long as they pleased, who have lived a purely spatial life and who wake up, in a transport of joy, and put on their shoes.

Moreover, in space, everything was too vulnerable. Space always left a mark, it could not be furnished. And everyone who passed by hit it as if it were a target.

Whereas out of my land once more . . .

Ah! that will revolutionize my life.

Mother always predicted absolute poverty and nullity for me. All right. So far, I admit, with the land as it was, she has been right; but now, we shall see what we shall see.

I was the despair of my parents, but just wait! And besides, I shall be happy. There will always be lots of folk around. Sometimes, you know, I used to be very lonely.

('Mes Propriétés')   (*Translated by James Kirkup*)

ENIGMAS

for Jules Supervielle

THEY know what it is to wait. I knew one of them, and others knew him too, who used to wait. He had put himself into a hole and was waiting.

Now if you were looking for a hole for something or other, believe me, it would be better if you looked elsewhere, and for some other hole; or else sat down beside him, smoking the long pipes of patience.

For he never left his hole.

People threw stones at him, and he ate them.

He would look surprised, then he would eat them. Sleeping and waking, he would remain where he was, longer than it takes a prejudice to die, longer than the life of a cedar, longer than the psalms sung by fallen cedars; he just went on waiting, growing gradually less and less until he was no more than the shadow of his big toe.

. . .

I was busy moulding a little animal, a sort of mouse, out of a pellet of bread. I had barely finished its third paw when suddenly it began to run . . . I ran right away, under cover of darkness.

('Qui Je Fus', 1927)   (*Translated by James Kirkup*)

Paul Eluard

SUITE

To sleep, with the moon in one eye and the sun in the
    other,
With love in one's mouth, and a bright bird in one's hair,
Gay as the fields, the woods, the highways and the sea,
    Beautiful and gay as a ride round the world.

       Fly into the landscape
Among the branches of smoke and all the fruits of the wind,
    Legs of stone in stockings of sand,
    A neat waist with all a river's muscles
    And the final worry on a transformed face.

('Répétitions')   *(Translated by James Kirkup)*

Paul Eluard

THE NIGHT

CARESS the horizon of night, seek for the heart of jet that dawn covers over with flesh. It would put innocent thoughts into your eyes, flames, wings and green leaves that were not invented by the sun. It is not night you miss, but its power.

('Nouveaux Poèmes')   (*Translated by James Kirkup*)

SHE is—but not until midnight, when all the white birds have closed their wings over the ignorance of darkness, when the sister of the myriads of pearls has hidden her two hands in her dead hair, when the triumphant is pleased to weep, weary of his services to curiosity, male and brilliant armour of luxury. She is so gentle that she has transfigured my heart. I was afraid of the great shadows that weave the cloth of card-tables and fine clothes, I was afraid of the sun's contortions at evening, of the unbreakable branches that purify the windows of all the confessionals where sleeping women wait for us.

O bust of memory, error of form, absent lines, flame extinguished in my shut eyes, I stand before your grace like a child in water, like a bunch of flowers in a forest. The nocturnal universe moves in your warmth and the towns of yesterday make street-gestures more delicate than the hawthorn, more surprising than the time. The earth in the distance breaks into unmoving smiles, the sky envelopes life: a new star of love rises from everywhere—finished, there are no other proofs of night.

('Nouveaux Poèmes')   (*Translated by James Kirkup*)

To come back to a city of velvet and porcelain, the windows will be vases where the flowers, having left the earth, will show what light really is.

To see silence, to give it a kiss on the lips, and the roofs of the city will be beautiful melancholy birds with fleshless wings.

To love no longer anything but gentleness and immobility with its marble eye, its pearly forehead, its dreaming eye, its living forehead, its hands that, without ever closing, hold everything in their scales, the most reliable in the world, never varying and always correct.

Man's heart will blush no more, he will be lost no longer, I come back, out of myself, out of all eternity.

('Nouveaux Poèmes')   (*Translated by James Kirkup*)

Jean Cocteau

BATTERY

Sun, I adore you like a savage,
flat on my belly by the river.

Sun, you burnisher of brasses, gild
your baskets full of fruit, your animals.

Make my body brown and salt;
Make my great hurt go away.

The negro, whose teeth are white,
is black outside, and pink within.

But I am pink outside and black
within: make the exchange.

Change me in odour and in colour,
as you changed Hyacinth into a flower.

Let the cicada in the pine-tops bray,
and make me smell of new-baked bread.

The tree at noonday filled with night
at evening spreads it out beside him.

Make me spread out my evil dreams,
sun, serpent of Adam and of Eve.

Make me a little more resigned
to my poor friend Jean being killed.

Lottery, pile up your prizes
of balls and knives and vases.

You display your pinchbeck wares
to the wild beasts, to the Antilles.

For us, bring out the best you have
so as not to hurt our eyes.

Fat Lady, roundabout
of velvet, mirrors and arpeggios,

Tear out my hurt, pull hard,
charlatan with the golden cart.

How hot I am! It is noon.
I no longer know what I am saying.

My shadow is no more around me,
sun! menagerie of the months.

Sun, Buffalo Bill, Barnum,
you excite me more than opium.

You are a clown, a toreador,
you have watch-chains made of gold.

You are a dark-blue negro who boxes
the equators, the equinoxes.

Sun, I can bear your blows;
your great punches on my neck.

You are the one I am in love with still,
sun, delicious hell.

(Translated by James Kirkup)

Jules Supervielle

REGRET FOR EARTH

The day will come when we shall say: 'That was the time
Of the sun. Do you remember its light on the tiniest branch,
How it surprised a girl, and fell on an old woman,
And the moment it rested on things gave them their colour?
It followed the horse's gallop and stopped still when he
    stopped.
That was the unforgettable time of our stay on Earth,
When if a thing was dropped it made a noise in falling,
We used to gaze around with eyes of comprehension,
And our ears understood each slight change in the air,
And when our dear friend's step came near to us we knew it;
It might be a flower we picked up or a polished stone,
That was the time when we couldn't catch the smoke,
Alas! That's all that our hands could capture now.'

(Translated by James Kirkup)

IT

It must not be spoken
Nor even murmured.
It must not be written,
It must not be dreamed of
Even in delirium,
It must not be looked at
Except with bandaged eyes
And above all it must not be approached
Except with gloves of iron.

. . . . . .

At the hour when day
Despairing of evening
Is about to cover its head
With its dark apron,
What do you want with me,
Presences, speak softly,
We might be overheard
And I be sold to death:
Cover my face
With boughs of green
And let me be mingled
With the shadow of the world.

(Translated by James Kirkup)

FOR A DEAD POET

Quickly give him an ant,
Never mind if it's small
But let it be really his!
For a dead man mustn't be tricked.
Give him that for himself, or perhaps a swallow's beak,
A bit of grass, a bit of Paris.
All he has of his own is one great void
And he still can't properly understand his lot.

In exchange he gives you the choice
Of dimmer presents that the hand can't grasp:
A reflexion lying under the snow,
The top side of the highest of clouds,
Silence in the midst of chatter
Or the unprotected star.
All these things he names and gives you,
Lacking a dog or a human being himself.

(Translated by J. M. Cohen)

St. John Perse

from 'RAINS VII'

'Innumerable are our ways and our dwellings uncertain.
Whose lip is of clay quenches his thirst in the infinite.
You who wash the dead in the mother-waters of the
morning—and the world is still entangled in the
bramble-bush of war-wash as well as the faces of the
living: wash, oh Rains, the melancholy faces of the
violent, the gentle faces of the violent . . . for their
ways are restricted and their dwellings uncertain.

Wash, oh Rains! a place of stone for the strong. At
tremendous tables beneath the pent-roof of their
strength, there will sit those who have not been in-
toxicated by the wine of men, those who have not been
sullied by a tendency to tears or to dreams, those who
are indifferent to their names in trumpets of bone . . .
at tremendous tables will they sit, beneath the pent-
roof of their strength, in a place of stone for the strong.

Wash doubt and prudence from the steps of action, wash
doubt and propriety from the field of vision. Wash the
leucoma from the eyes of the man of good taste, from
the eye of the man of good tone; the leucoma of the
man of merit, the leucoma of the man of talent; wash
the scales from the eye of the Master and the mycenas,
from the eye of those who are law-abiding, and influential . . . from the eye of men who are qualified by
propriety and by prudence.

Wash, wash benevolence from the heart of the great Intercessors, seemliness from the brows of great Educationalists, and the contamination of language from public

lips. Wash, oh Rains, the hand of the Judge and the Provost, the hand of the midwife and the layer-out, the licked hands of blind men and of cripples, and the sordid hand, upon men's brows, that dreams repeatedly of reins and whip . . . with the consent of the great Intercessors, and the great Educationalists.

Wash, wash whole histories of peoples from the lofty tables of memory: the great official annals, the great chronicles of the Clergy and the academic bulletins. Wash the bulls and the charters, and the Records of the Tiers-Etat; the Covenants, the Treaties of alliance and the great federative bonds; wash, wash, oh Rains! all the vellums and the parchments, coloured like walls of asylums and leper settlements, colours of fossilised ivory and the yellow teeth of old rulers . . . Wash, wash, oh Rains! the lofty tables of memory.

Oh Rains! wash from the heart of man his most wonderful sayings: his loveliest sentences, his loveliest sequences; the best-turned phrases, the best-born pages. Wash, wash from the heart of men their taste for cantilenæ, and for elegies; their taste for vilanelles and rondeaux; their great felicities of expression; wash the salt of atticism and the honey of euphemism, wash, wash the bedding of dreams and the straw of knowledge: from the heart of the man who never refuses, from the heart of the man who never condemns, wash, wash, oh Rains! the greatest gifts of man . . . from the hearts of the men who are most talented for the great works of reason.'

(Translated by Walford Morgan)

THE PRINCE'S FRIENDSHIP

EVERY season I will return, with a green loquacious bird upon my wrist. Friend of the silent Prince. And from the mouth of rivers my return will be announced. From him a letter is delivered me by the people on the coast:

'The Prince's friendship! Make haste . . . His estate perhaps to share. And his confidence, and favourite dish . . . I will await you every season at the highest tide-mark of the sea, questioning about your projects the sailor folk of sea and river . . . War, and trade, and the settlement of religious dues are usually the cause of people moving far away: but you are content to move long distances without a cause. I know this ferment of the spirit. I will explain to you the origin of your ill. Make haste.

And whether your perception has grown more keen is another thing I shall want to verify. And as the man, upon his journeying, who finds a tree of hives has the right to take the honey, I will gather in the fruit of your wisdom; and I will avail myself of your counsel. In the evenings of great drought upon the earth, we will discourse upon the things of the spirit. Things that are conclusive, and things uncertain. And we will rejoice in all the secrets that the spirit covets . . . But from one race to another the journey is long; and I have work to do elsewhere. Make haste! I am awaiting you! . . . Come by the lowland country and the camphor woods.'

So runs his letter. That of a wise man. And my reply is this:

'Honour to the Prince under his name! The condition of man is uncertain. And there are some who show some excellence. In the evenings of the great drought upon the earth, I have heard speak of you on this side of the world, and the praises were not meagre. Your name is as the shadow of a great tree. I speak of it sometimes to the dust-laden travellers on the roads; and they are refreshed.

This too I have to tell you:

I have received your message. And rejoice in your friendship as in a gift of odorous leaves: my heart is refreshed with it . . . Like the North-West wind when it drives the waters of the sea deeply into the rivers (and to find drinkable water one has to follow the course of the tributaries), a similar state of fortune leads me to you. And I will make haste, savouring in my mouth your stimulating leaf.'

That is my letter, closely written. And meanwhile He is waiting for me, seated in the cooling shadow near his doorway . . .

(Translated by Walford Morgan)

SONG

My horse having halted beneath a tree of turtle-doves, I whistle with my lips a whistling note so pure, that there are no promises upon their banks which the rivers do not keep (Animated leaves appear in the morning light as bright reflections of glory) . . .

And it is not that a man is not melancholy, but rising before day and standing prudently within the busy susurration of an ancient tree, and resting with his chin upon the last remaining star, he perceives in the depths of the fasting sky things of great loveliness and purity which minister joy . . .

My horse now halted beneath this dove-loud tree, I whistle with my lips a whistling note so pure . . .

. . . And peace to those, if they are about to die, who have not seen so wonderful a day. But from my brother the poet I have received some news. He has written yet another lovely thing. And some have made a note of it . . .

(Translated by Walford Morgan)

Aimé Césaire

THE WOMAN AND THE KNIFE

Flesh luxuriant to the teeth, O spirals pared from solid flesh
   fly into shivers of day, into splinters of night, into the
   light caress of winds, into stems of light, into the sterns
   of silence;
fly trapped entanglements, anvils of dark flesh, fly
fly into children's shoes, into silver fountains,
fly and defy the cataphracted creatures of night mounted
   upon their wild asses,
you birds,
you blood,
who has suggested I would not be there?
nor there my heart unannotated,
my heart without regret my heart annuitied,
and the giant forest trees of majestic rain?
Numbers, sacred jewels, eternal snows, icicles, and tourneys,
there will be pollens, moons, seasons with hearts of bread
   and bells
the tall furnaces of strike and impossibility will exude saliva,
bullets, choral societies, mitres, candelabra,
O dumb pandanus peopled with migrations
O blue Niles—O dwarf prayers—O my mother, O track
and the savage spattered heart
the greatest of thrilling terrors is still to flower
in vain.

(Translated by Walford Morgan)

THE SCAPEGOAT

The veins of the river-bank are numbed with strange larvæ
we and our brothers
in the fields the skeletons await their tremors and their flesh:
    nothing will come and the season is void
The gnat-bite of our promises is carried out above the
    breast of a village, and the village has died with all
    its men, who were only recognisable yesterday
    through their tubes of mica, by the violet
    patience of their silent excrements,
O twilight gleam,
so fragile, so fragile on the verge of night lies the
    pastry-shop of landscape that at the fine
    white-headed osprey's jubilation she flies thither
    but for the eye which is self-observant, there
    lies on the parapet prophetic of shadow and
    trembling at the whims of pyrites a heart
    which pumps a blood of light and grass.
And the sea, Arborigenus, a fistful of rumours
    between its teeth, drags itself out from its
    marsupial bones and placing its first island-stone
    in the wind which collapses from the renewed
    vigour of the foetus, dreams of setting light to
    its punchbowls of anthems and of mirage
    towards the naked miracle of our towns which reach
    out for the future and our clacking scape-goat jaws.

(Translated by Walford Morgan)

THE DUNGEONS OF THE SEA
AND OF THE FLOOD

Day O day of New York and of Soukala
I refer to you
to you who will be no more absurdly the sport of the
    death's-head sphinx or rebellious eczema,
and the day, quite simply, the day
takes off its gloves
its gloves of blue wind, of raw milk, and of salt,
its gloves of shark's egg calm and fire of black straw,
aridity
you were powerless against my aquiferous acorns,
the chemical ballet of unaccustomed worlds,
the powder of eyes finely crushed beneath the pestle,
seagulls immovably enamoured of spindles and water
create the inalterable alloy of my hourless sleep
hourless but for the geyser unappeasement of the tree
    of silence
hourless but for the fraternal catastrophe with its
    hair of hippocampus and campeachy wood
hourless but for my eyes of sisal and of cobweb
my eyes that are the key of the world and the debris of a
    daytime
where you can catch a fever mounted on 300,000 fireflies
hourless but for the knives of sun-rays flung abroad
    in great showers
around the neck-band of climates
hourless but for the birds which raid the mill-leets of the
    heavens to assuage their thirst-for-sleeping-in-the-flood
hourless but for the inconsolable bird-blood which,
    through waiting, flares up in the agriculture of your
    eyes to annul the fine weather,
hourless but for the fabulous voice of forests which
suddenly shake our their sails in the caulking-yards
    of marshland and of coke,
hourless but for the low-water mark of lunations in
the responsible brain of people fed with insults and
    millenaries,

hourless but alas! hourless but for your bull-like
    incorruptible phlegm
which never snows more salubrious and mortal an appeal
as when awake from rivulets on my bark
ear of corn and novena of disaster (the real one)
The woman
who upon her drinking lips lulls to sleep the palankeen
    of the dungeons of the sea.

(Translated by Walford Morgan)

Patrice de la Tour du Pin

THE WASHERWOMEN

You must have seen the trees, the tallest trees,
The wind playing at their crests amid the boughs,
Rain-laden usually, this soft South breeze
To join once more the further border's blowing;
If you lean to listen, you will hear it rouse,
Annie, for like a hound I scent, foretell
Storms which must fill my stream to overflowing:
We've no time now to beat ere vesper bell
The suds of a village which will disappear. . . .

We have no time now to escape: perhaps
Of this wild quest you have already learned,
Deep to the country of the sea to slide,
In this slight stream 'neath which can be discerned
Sweet figures, children's voices drifting past
And hamlets crying, now covered by the tide!

But 'tis no wind that cries in such a strain,
Instinctive terror should have taught us all:
The weirs have burst their banks, dead waters drain
Sweeping before us, panting, clasp the drowned:
Annie, I beg you, do not curse my stream,
'Tis all the vale in winter, eddying round
To quiver with perpetual shuddering cry:
Annie, 'tis much more than one lone boat-washhouse
Drifting so slow one thinks it motionless,
Before our eyes now, sliding ghosts process
While the winds toss your hair against the sky!

The noise of rising tides is in your ears,
We are being swept on in the current's race:

You will re-live the legend which one hears
At dusk, in villages the storm maroons:
A wooden house drifting towards the sea,
Passing with songs and crazy laughing loons,
Never in this bare valley seen again. . . .

Annie, can you remember such a battle
Of wind before? Swelled by so many low
Far cries from hamlets seized by flood, the cattle
Stampeding in a fear you cannot know:
They have all fled, with men, to high hills bare,
A whole world, motionless, marooned, who stand
And thence gaze down at my stream flooding, where
Two souls sweep past without the will to land!

We are, of living souls, the lone, the last
The tides permit to meddle with illusion,
Recover in their marvellous confusion
Loved scenes, made magical by being past,
The grassy fields each, individual, known,
And hamlets, fireless, in the moonlight shown
Where prowls the terror of the midnight grave!

And we'll pass on where other hamlets stand,
Speeding before the all-destructive wave,
To see the fields lost on a winter's night,
And frosted dawns where ends the living land,

And in the sunrise, the first seagulls' flight. . . .

(*Translated by M. K. Howorth*)

TWO POEMS OF CALSEHENNE

It takes the breeze well, my young tree,
He takes life well who bends his head,
Better than I, who have no roots
Elsewhere than in the here and now:
One lacks time to grow into it.
The rest is slow in ripening,
One can reckon the body's age,
But should I find another field
Between my childhood and my death?

(*Translated by J. M. Cohen*)

The sound of his voice passes us by,
His countryside is never ours.
By listening and pondering
We sometimes think we understand him;
But we can never answer questions
About his music or his language:
So what good does he get by singing?
—At least you have a paradise,
At least you have a clearing,
At least you have a glance or two
To toss on like a boat at sea,
At least you have a dark ravine,
Inevitably your own hell.
What I have is little more,
But the wide open gulf of sky,
There all the joy of being alive
Laments and cries aloud and soars;
It's there that creatures must be friends,
Since but one human secret's mine,
A friend from sharing the same hope.

(*Translated by J. M. Cohen*)